Praise for *This Body Is Never at Rest*

This Body Is Never at Rest is an exhilarating ride that has its own momentum; it's Poe's heart beating incessantly; it's a Camus-like existential dread; it's a rational twist of an individual caught in the everlasting, universe's turning motion, a psychological thriller. The cadences have a comforting certainty. Bart Edelman writes, "Now you must heal yourself / Through the sorrow grace dictates, / When the heart's song / Longs to sing again." It's an acceptance of love to face the oncoming night. It's a daring, maddening, joyful journey. Hang on!

> Harry E. Northup, *Love Poem to MPTF*

The thoughtful and charming poems in *This Body Is Never at Rest* explore the terrain between the page and the world. Erasmus and Mark Twain are as likely to show up as James Dean and Walter White. But just as often, the poet wanders away from other texts, to behold the stars, the airplanes, and the quiet lives of strangers. In Bart Edelman's work, curiosity is the highest of virtues, wonder the greatest of all pleasures.

> Tyler McMahon, *One Potato*, and Editor, *Hawaii Pacific Review*

Bart Edelman's new and selected collection of poetry, *This Body Is Never at Rest*, covers thirty years of poems ranging from the sublime in "This Body Is Never at Rest," "Although the Holy Spirit is asleep / Although the universe cries, Foul," to the mundane in "Voice of America," "Someone's calling my cell phone / But I don't recognize the number." Throughout this honed collection, one finds the ebb and flow of life as in "If Only I Could," "Because you threatened me with love / Escape became my sole exit . . . / Surely, you'll find another more worthy, / Who's been seeking someone like you / To provide them a stable life— / Structure and form I eschew. / All that remains is the truth: / I would love you, if only I could." With echoes of the delicate balance of life, love, and work, the collection makes one more aware of the fragility of contentment to the point of "Despair," "I am done with despair— / Decided to cross it off." However, life brings moments of joy as in "Courtship," "But you said I was being silly. / Then I asked you to marry me, / And you said, yes, of course." And as in "The Open Window," "you / Pour a cup of tea, / Lean towards awakening," the faithful reader realizes life is filled with love, and this work of poetry solidifies it.

Robert L. Giron, *Songs for the Spirit*, and Editor, *ArLiJo*

Praise for *Whistling to Trick the Wind*

These poems are set against a universe where life is often meaningless except for the fact that Fate has "cooked the dice." Edelman's dealing with this plight ranges from surrealistic comedy and wordplay, to somber eulogy, to romantic love poem—all of which are delivered with reader-friendly wit, craftsmanship, and intelligence. The book finally moves from wry humor as a means of coping to the lifesaving power of awareness and love. An especially moving reflection of that shift is a recasting of Thomas' famous villanelle, in which Edelman says to his dying mother, "Good women watch each wave and see how bright / Their deeds have danced across a silver bay." *Whistling to Trick the Wind* is a voyage well worth taking.

William Trowbridge, Poet Laureate of Missouri (2012-2016), *Vanishing Point*

"Yes, let's raise a toast to the weary," welcome each other to this era's new Theater of the Absurd, filled with home-spun alienation, "nothing but hocus pocus," existential angst, and a beautiful deadpan delivery of the past, "One crime at a time." Who better to "stir the pot," to come knocking down the door of confusion, than poet Bart Edelman? Not the "proverbial rat," the "metonymist (who) killed time with a spoon," and certainly not you or your "faithful monkey." In his latest book, *Whistling to Trick the Wind*, Edelman has "nothing to confess but sorrow" and everything to confess regarding our future's brew and thaw of joy. This wonderful book reads like a contemporary film script, an adult bildungsroman, fragile "as a pennywhistle thistle / Caught in a terrible wind" and yet robust and blessed as that overhead "blanket of stars" that just might save us from ourselves.

Elena Karina Byrne, *If This Makes You Nervous*

With the sharpened blade of a consummate craftsman, along with a razor wit, Edelman pens another volume of poetry, perhaps his most intimate, and perhaps the collection that delves most deeply into his irresistible characters' lives: a magician, an Uber driver, a presidential candidate, a broken lover, many others. Always engaging, always close and familiar, Edelman continues to shine brightly, especially so in this new collection, *Whistling to Trick the Wind*. Read it. Enjoy. It will bring you light, too.

Kevin Rabas, Poet Laureate of Kansas (2017-2019), *More Than Words*

In *Whistling to Trick the Wind*, Bart Edelman asks us to look at the world differently. In the opening poem, "The Woodpecker," the speaker confides, "I ask myself what I've done / To earn admission into heaven." The poems that follow explore the challenges life brings with honesty and wry humor. In "Maude Tells Claude," Edelman invites the reader to "Slowly place one foot / In front of the other." That act of slow reflection is at the center of "Truth or Consequence" as we ponder "How possible is it / To heal the heart." Ultimately, it is our heart that has grown as we take the time to read and wonder about and revel in Edelman's poems.

Jill Gerard, Editor, *Chautauqua*

Bart Edelman's *Whistling to Trick the Wind* captures the dilemma of humanity's timeless struggle—the desire to be free in a world full of constraints, sometimes external, but also habitually internal. Edelman has managed to create a world that is both unique and yet precisely our own, where, as the speaker of "Revolution" proclaims, "the only name you know / For uncertainty is fate." As our journey with the poet continues, we must ask ourselves, like the speaker in "Collapsing City," whether we really are just "men and women / Gripped tightly in nature's

fist / Unable to claim reason / As anything more than chance—"
or if the answer perhaps lies somewhere else, as our "future is
cast / In never-ending chapters / Of truth or consequence." This
is a masterfully crafted collection from beginning to end.

David Garyan, Assistant Editor, *Interlitq*

Bart Edelman's poems are searching and direct testaments from
a poet who understands the sadness of the everyday, and savors
its small victories. *Whistling to Trick the Wind* is a book full of
close observation and wry humor, but also of gratitude and
tenderness, exemplified by the strange tale of bowtie salesman
Solomon Schwartz in "Towards Sleep," and by "Go Gentle into
That Good Night," a tribute to Dylan Thomas's villanelle, which
Edelman turns into a poem about acceptance, and a moving
farewell.

Charles Harper Webb, *Sidebend World*

Praise for *The Geographer's Wife*

The way magnetism draws the needle of a compass, yearning
pulls the poems in this collection through the cardinal directions
of a world in which time is not linear but circular, cyclical.
Hunger draws lost loved ones to the table, calls lovers away from
home and onto the open road. A peculiarly American manifest
destiny directs Colonel Sanders to proselytize chicken trinity
to the streets, while Raggedy Ann rips her stockings and aches
for danger. Quirky characters, popular culture, and memory
align here in a topography at once hilarious and haunting. Bart
Edelman's *The Geographer's Wife* orients the reader in the body
as a map of desire, where the individual life becomes a locus of
its own, a point from which the world demarcates itself.

Amy Sage Webb, Editor, *Flint Hills Review*

Bart Edelman understands how words should taste, how sounds
strung with precision can create a universe of meaning far beyond
denotation. These poems are etched into mirrors—transparent,

but with surprises built to stand up through reading after reading. You will see your reflection smiling back in recognition on every page. With a cast of characters ranging from acrobats on speed to lumberjacks with wings, *The Geographer's Wife* is an accomplished collection.

Tom Chandler, Poet Laureate of Rhode Island emeritus

Bart Edelman's sixth book, *The Geographer's Wife*, is chock-full of stunning, stand-out poems. In "Holiday," the poet explores the soulful textures of loss present in the first Mother's Day after his mother has passed. In another, the poet compares modern dating to "The New Math," a system that has changed so profoundly as to make the addition of romance nearly impossible. In this collection, Bart Edelman is single-minded in his purpose. He takes in the popular language of America—East, North, South and West—and creates buoyant melodies of "coolness," a popular verbal chill that also diagnoses our deepest troubles—contemporary isolation and a profound longing for love.

Todd James Pierce, *Newsworld*, winner of the Drue Heinz Literary Prize

I fell in love on first reading *The Geographer's Wife*. It promises and delivers—such riches to follow. Then I met Uncle Irv from "The Contiguous 48" and was taken, forever. In this wonderful and wide-ranging collection of poems, Bart Edelman charts the elusive latitudes and longitudes of desire. With antic humor and often rueful insight, he takes the reader on an emotional journey through time and space. So leave your suitcase and your fears behind, pick up your compass and open the door. Adventure awaits!

Elizabeth Forsythe Hailey, *A Woman of Independent Means*

Praise for *The Last Mojito*

Bart Edelman's *The Last Mojito* weaves passionate poetic portraits into a cohesive, enthralling collection. These poems represent an astonishing range of vision and connect to the tradition of American literature as they artfully remind us of Edwin Arlington Robinson's sonnets and Sherwood Anderson's "The Book of the Grotesque."

> Ryan G. Van Cleave, *Contemporary American Poetry: Behind the Scenes* and *The Longman Anthology of Poetry*

The poems in Bart Edelman's *The Last Mojito* offer us a modest, straight-faced take on a surreal landscape that is recognizably our own, from "Little Daddy's Thanksgiving" visit to the troops to the humble sanctification of "The Potato." It's a world where "The dog is not your friend," so it's "Better to stick with the snake." Drawn in by the poems' rhythms of plausibility, and by their unexpected detail, we find ourselves assenting to the wry vision with a resigned acceptance akin to that of the poet.

> Sandra Kohler, *The Country of Women* and *The Ceremonies of Longing*

Bart Edelman is one of my favorite poets—spare and smart, lyrical but never sentimental about the mechanics of love. In this new collection, *The Last Mojito*, he invokes figures both public and private to get at the "long drawn-out sorrow" of our silent hearts. Edelman is an elegist, writing laments for our daily losses and capitulations, yet seeing hope where, by all rights, it should not exist. In the process, he continually exposes the difficult dynamics of what it means to be human.

> David L. Ulin, *Another City: Writing from Los Angeles* and *Writing Los Angeles: A Literary Anthology*

Shouldn't a poem make something happen? What would it be like, a poem that makes you sweat, bare your teeth, flush with blood, tear up, emit sharp sounds? Perhaps something like the lines of these poems in *The Last Mojito*—elegant, slim knives that prick the reader into dark or bright laughter. With humor and a sly simplicity, Bart Edelman's imagination, broad as the Great Plains, carries us from the ghosts of slaughtered buffalo to the president's "lovesick missile" to teach us the "apocryphal lessons" of lust and politics. He cuts us a bit in the process. And yes, we bleed.

Tony Barnstone, *The Anchor Book of Chinese Poetry* and *The Art of Writing: Teachings of the Chinese*

Praise for *The Gentle Man*

Not quite like any other poetry I've read . . . Bart Edelman's complex and inexhaustible song in *The Gentle Man* concerns his admission that "What I really know about love / Could never amount to much." With this as a given, we experience a poetry of "ultimate shadow": lovers only playing house, ghosts arriving at our front doors, lovers simultaneously stealing and giving. The gentle man yearns for a bat's instinct of echolocation so that he can steer clear of misery, but collides with walls of desire and loss that seem part of our inner-architecture. Reading this unexpected, unusual, troubling book, I kept thinking of Emerson's "Up again, old heart!" And my deep anxieties were answered with poetry.

William Heyen, *Erika: Poems of the Holocaust*

So much in our life asks us to speed up, to charge ahead. These poems ask something else—take some time here, and then come back and sit again. Thankfully, the subsequent visits are worth the effort.

Eloise Klein Healy, *Passing*

Praise for *The Alphabet of Love*

Often humorous, always tender-hearted, Bart Edelman is the best kind of poet we have: he doesn't talk low to the masses, and he doesn't talk pretentious for the esoteric few. Call him a poet for an elite readership—an elite, however, that encompasses an immense public who love literature. "Twelve black pearls / Sang to me" he writes in one poem. But this entire collection of shimmering pearls sings to a multitude of grateful readers when they spell out, poem by poem, *The Alphabet of Love.*

Oscar Mandel, *Fundamentals of the Art of Poetry*

All of the tightly woven, passionate lines in Bart Edelman's *The Alphabet of Love* enter your heart, where they cast a hypnotic spell that leaves you with new insights about love ("The Locket"), hate ("Little Ghosts"), despair ("Footsteps"), and even whimsy ("The Alphabet of Love"). Edelman has made a significant contribution to contemporary poetry by using language—figurative and literal—that lays bare the paradoxes and ironies of human pain and joy.

Jo Ray McCuen, *Readings for Writers*

Bart Edelman's are elegant lean poems that penetrate directly to the heart of human life.

Miriam Sagan, *Archeology of Desire*

Praise for *Under Damaris' Dress*

Edelman manages to catch our darkest fantasies and secrets and grudging loves with grace and wit. His poetry also honors love and the erotic . . . a very promising poet.

Stephen Minot, *Three Genres*

Bart Edelman's poetry is true art. These beautiful knowing poems are about loneliness, love, and isolation, poems which have at their center a stillness as well as a strong presence.

Cheri Davis Langdell, *WS Merwin*

Edelman's poetry shows an artist at work. Always in control of his craft, Edelman lets the humor, the fear, and the humanity involved in any person's life shine through. . . . His poetry is touching, poignant, metaphoric and breathtaking.

Mike Cluff, *Inside English*

Bart Edelman's work delves into the wonderment of childhood and the uncertainty of aging.

Rick Holguin, *Los Angeles Times*

Praise for *Crossing the Hackensack*

Bart Edelman bridges the two worlds of scholarly poetry and the oral traditions of street poetry to create a rich work of art which touches the reader on many levels. His poetry appeals not only to the intellect but also to the emotions.

Michael Logue, *Steel and Ivy*, Chapman University

Edelman has written movingly about the cultural and emotional limbo of living abroad.

Susan Heeger, *Los Angeles Times*

Meadowlark Press, LLC
meadowlarkbookstore.com
P.O. Box 333, Emporia, KS 66801

This Body Is Never at Rest: New and Selected Poems 1993 - 2023
Copyright © Bart Edelman 2024
www.bartedelman.com

This book uses Calibri and Felix Titling fonts.

Ordering Information: Special discounts are available on quantity purchases by corporations, associations, and others. For details, contact the publisher at info@meadowlark-books.com.

Cover Photo: Carolyn Ellsworth Henley
Cover Design: Austin Doyle, www.austindennisdoyle.com
Book Design: Susan Cisco and Linzi Garcia

POETRY / American / General
POETRY / Subjects & Themes / General
POETRY / Subjects & Themes / Places

ISBN: 978-1-956578-56-0 Hardback
ISBN: 978-1-956578-55-3 Paperback
ISBN: 978-1-956578-57-7 E-Book

Library of Congress Control Number: 2023951503

THIS BODY IS NEVER AT REST

NEW AND SELECTED POEMS
1993 – 2023

BART EDELMAN

MEADOWLARK PRESS
Celebrating 10 Years
established 2014
EMPORIA, KANSAS

for Beatrice, Kim, and Susan

THIS BODY IS NEVER AT REST

NEW AND SELECTED POEMS
1993 – 2023

POEMS

THIS BODY IS NEVER AT REST

MORNING

AFTERNOON

EVENING

WHISTLING TO TRICK THE WIND

THE GEOGRAPHER'S WIFE

THE LAST MOJITO

THE GENTLE MAN

THE ALPHABET OF LOVE

UNDER DAMARIS' DRESS

CROSSING THE HACKENSACK

THIS BODY IS NEVER AT REST

MORNING

THIS BODY IS NEVER AT REST

This body is never at rest:
For reasons I now suspect,
For what it may portend,
For where the next breath leads,
For steps of jubilant agony.

This body is never at rest:
Although it yearns for repair,
Although an avalanche awaits,
Although the Holy Spirit is asleep,
Although the universe cries, *Foul*.

This body is never at rest:
Despite forgetting its last name,
Despite working 'round the clock,
Despite a simple state of decency,
Despite the hatchet in its back pocket.

This body is never at rest:
Hence the clarion call to arms,
Hence a thought in a glass bottle,
Hence each muscle at mid twitch,
Hence no date of expiration.

This body is never at rest:
Because the morning is an uncoiled string,
Because the afternoon pays no taxes,
Because the evening needs a shadow,
Because this body says so.

ERASMUS

You had to know Erasmus,
To get the get of him,
My mother would often say.
He was an eccentric, large, black dog,
By the time I came along—
What with three older brothers
Who chased him, unmercifully,
Through the plentiful thickets,
Surrounding our house outside the swamps,
Comprising Teaneck, at that time.
I think when he saw me
He realized, he was, happily,
In for a rather easy time of it
And would lie for hours at my feet,
Dreaming of other dogs—or what not.

While my questionable social disorder—
Or any number of other maladies—
Limited my close friendships,
Erasmus constantly tailed me,
As if I were king of the universe.
It was only in his untimely passing—
He chased a car that stopped
When he made contact with it—
I felt grief for the first time
And deeply languished in it,
For what seemed to be an eternity.
Now, I still desire unconditional love,
But the mere thought of Erasmus,
Barking to his heart's content,
Brings me such utter joy,
I can barely contain myself.

Bart Edelman

THE SYSTEM

We tried to run the system—
The way we'd been taught—
But it just wouldn't work,
No matter what we did.
We consulted the latest manual,
In, at least, nine languages,
Phoned a support hotline,
Scheduled an expensive home visit,
Yet, utterly, to no avail.
We were at our wits' end.
If there was anything, whatsoever,
We'd been able to count on—
Year after year after year—
It was, certainly, the system,
And how, indeed, it represented
The state of the art,
In all its various manifestations,
Despite prevailing notions, regarding
A population hell-bent on change.
Sadly, then, with much misgiving,
We took it upon ourselves
To undo what was once done—
Dismantle the entire operation,
Until it simply failed to exist.
Even we couldn't recognize it,
After we made our final decision,
Sending it spinning into the heap.
Nowadays, there's a befitting silence,
Waiting to greet us each morning.
I guess it comes with the territory—
This end of the cycle,
As we well know it.

FLIGHT 1903

My ass hat seatmate, in 17B,
Complains, endlessly, about the flight.
Drones on and on and on,
Regarding the inadequate meal service,
The shoddy condition of the aircraft,
And the crew's general ineptitude.
I attempt to feign sleep deprivation—
Doze off at a moment's notice—
Snore loudly if need be—
But he'll have none of it.
He constantly engages me in blather,
Until I retreat to the restroom,
For nothing more than basic relief.

What's worse, we're only an hour
Into this LA>NY cross country trek,
And because the plane is full,
I've nowhere else to go—
A prisoner, as it were, I'm afraid—
Caught, like a convict, in 17A.
Oh well, I try and rationalize;
It's not the LA>Cairo exhaustive trip
I remember taking many years ago.
Yes, 23 hours, trapped in the sky,
With this gas clown and a half,
Would surely make me wish
The Wright brothers had been wrong.

Bart Edelman

OUT OF THE COUNTRY

Out of the country—
For as long as I dare remember;
My return caused nothing of a stir.
No one I knew came to the station
When I disembarked from the train,
Whose destination remained a mystery,
All those swollen, uncontested years
I traveled, track to track.

At first, I stood on the platform,
Attempting to recognize my surroundings.
A stranger approached and asked,
Why the long, sad face?
I told him I was born that way.
He simply shrugged his shoulders,
Appeared to straggle away,
Whistling the national anthem.

Moments later, I collected my valise—
Empty as an owl on a fencepost—
And considered my options.
Since there were none available,
I was forced to choose the latter.
One step quickly led to another.
I followed a rather crooked path
In whatever direction the night allowed.

Where I ultimately came to settle
Appeared to be as good as any other.
The town has a distinct name,

But I am not aware of it.
The place could feel like home—
If only I had a change of clothes.
Perhaps, one day I may discover
How life is meant to be lived.

PACIFIC SURFLINER

The train was always traveling—
But it never stopped for us.
We watched the Pacific Surfliner,
As it wound its way, due north,
To Oxnard, Ventura, and Santa Barbara,
Leaving us in the lurch.
One day, one day, one day,
We whispered repeatedly, longingly,
Waiting for tomorrow to board
The ride of our dreams.
We listened to the iconic horn,
Tempting us far and away,
While we climbed up the bank,
Just to get a glimpse of freedom—
Drawing closer and closer—
Gliding smoothly down the track.
It was all we could do to keep
From flinging ourselves, frenzy-like,
Smack-dab towards the locomotive.
Along the rail's path we sped,
Chasing a non-existent ticket
We were forced to purchase—
The very notion of escape:
Impractical, improbable, impossible.
Only in the cab car's waning shadow
Did we suppose a time might arrive,
When we were worthy enough to hear
The conductor welcome us aboard,
Announce each scheduled destination—
One future route after another.

SOMEONE LIKE GODOT

I, too, have been waiting
For someone like Godot—
Or a fellow who looks similar,
Despite my lack of awareness,
Concerning who he must really be.
Listen, it just appears obvious—
If you're taking your chances—
To err on Providence's side,
Until you know any better.
And, even then, I imagine,
It could be too late to change
What is your ultimate fate,
Wherever direction you're headed.

Perhaps, it's the aimless who succeed,
Without a rudder in the water.
They cast no net to speak of,
Relying only upon a vision—
A whim, if you will—
Simply put, the choice one makes,
When nothing certain remains.
It's as good a place as any
To hang the oversized hat you wear,
Keeping the rain at bay.
Yes, I'll place my money on Godot;
He seems rather harmless—
Ready for the task at hand.

THE PIED PIPER

When we pied the piper, last spring;
He was less than pleased.
Seemed he'd definitely had it
With this current gig of his.
He wanted to trade in his flute,
Seek new employment possibilities,
Pursue more lucrative work,
As long as it didn't involve rats—
Or rodents of any kind, whatsoever.
Children were, of course, another matter.

Once he'd cleaned the meringue
Off his tired, weather-beaten face,
We felt sorry for our cruel actions
And ordered him a cold beer,
Which he downed in nothing flat.
He was one very thirsty dude,
Who kept drinking and drinking,
Halfway through the night—
While we kept him afloat.

In the morning we woke him up
And told him he'd best be on his way—
For a host of obvious reasons.
We begged him not to reveal
How we'd surely contributed
To the previous evening's debauchery.
He shrugged, took it in stride,
Grabbed his flute and was gone,
By the time we ate breakfast.

Today, the piper's whereabouts are a mystery.
The rumor mill is rife with reports,
Though none appear to be reputable.
The town's divided, left and right,
Wondering if he originally got a raw deal;
You know, with the rats and all—
And then not being paid for his services.
I guess that would piss me off, too.
A majority of the parents remain sore,
But it makes sense given the circumstances.

THE MAN WITHOUT A NAME

Everyone thought they knew him;
Everywhere he went he was recognized.
They misjudged him for a banker,
A lawyer, a professor, a car dealer,
A yachtsman, a restauranteur, a carpenter,
And a movie star, among countless others.
Folks would often sidle up to him,
Begin conversations, serious or jovial.
And he would befriend them, warmly,
As if he'd engaged them for years,
Even though he was a man
Without so much as a name—
Who was never asked to reveal it.
Had he been questioned, just once,
He would not have known how to respond.

The people who met him in Los Angeles,
Thought he was an Angeleno;
Those who greeted him in Boston,
Took him for a Bostonian.
He seemed at home on either coast—
A fellow for whom location was secondary.
He blended in like the frothy margarita
He ordered wherever he appeared to be.
Total strangers claimed he was a relative,
Although they were always a bit uncertain,
As to which side of the family he belonged.
The day after he disappeared,
He left sorrowful souls behind,
Who told endless stories about his exploits—
None of them real . . . all of them true.

THE GIRL

He had to knuckle down
And get it together.
If he were a train,
He'd be off the tracks,
Headed due south by Sunday.
It was, rather simply,
A matter of the girl—
That she had thrown him,
So far, so fast,
And he hadn't seen it coming
From such a short distance.

He had lost himself,
Somewhere in her world:
The bangles, the buttons, the braids.
Now, she was gone,
Leaving him with an emptiness
He completely failed to fill,
Each moment of every hour,
And hope was a four-letter word
He dared not repeat,
For fear struck him stock-still.

He wished he had never met her,
Been charmed by the shy kisses,
Kept his heart in check,
Given her a second thought.
But that was part of a past
He could not merely undo,
And he knew, for certain,
The very image of the girl,
Haunted the vacant stations
He visited day and night.

Bart Edelman

RESURRECTION

The resurrection was not my idea.
I wanted no part of it, at first.
But Ivan can be persuasive,
And after a few Mai Tai's—
Followed by copious amounts of beer—
I agreed to let him have his way,
Help raise Jimmy's blessed soul
Up through the stratosphere;
Then, the dear boy was on his own.

We planned the prank for a week,
Carefully making sure, of course,
Jimmy was on ice, as they say,
And available for the big event.
He died, after a prolonged illness—
His passing, in fact, a blessing.
We didn't want to startle his widow, Babs,
With the plan we had in store,
Just hoping she'd be fine,
Keeping to the original funeral date,
So we could claim Jimmy, early,
Avoiding the more traditional send-off.

Ivan enlisted Leo to engineer
The mechanical aspects of flight,
Once we launched Jimmy from *Sophie's* roof—
A bar where he had great success,
And quite a bit of notoriety.
I let the boys discuss aeronautical details,
As well as the launching technique.
I knew, full well, or hoped,
Jimmy wouldn't need to experience

The fire's thrust beneath him,
Catapulting him to touch the face of God.
But who can be absolutely certain?

Hours before our celebration,
I had fierce dreams throughout the night.
However, I attributed them all
To a severe case of the willies.
When dawn broke, the next morning,
I was surprised to find the police knocking,
Rather loudly, on my front door.
Seems Ivan's erratic wife, Mabel,
Found a copy of our plans, in a desk drawer,
And threatened him with a divorce
She'd been considering for the past year.

Needless to say, Ivan spilled the beans.
Immediately, Mabel phoned Babs.
Babs, in turn, contacted the police, hysterical,
And, voila, our mission was foiled,
Before we could send dear Jimmy skyward.
Luckily, we were never charged, criminally,
Because we hadn't fulfilled the act,
We bought all the products legally,
And, thank God, Ivan's cousin, Ernie,
Still was a lieutenant on the force,
Who vouched for each of us—
A kind and considerate measure.

Babs, on the other hand, was not as gracious.
She never quite treated us the same, again.
I gather, though, she had her reasons.

Bart Edelman

TUNNEL OF LOVE

Born in *The Tunnel of Love*—
Palisades Amusement Park, July, 1961.
Mother did not wait for ride's end,
Dispensing me by darkness,
On the metal floor of the car,
Before I could witness light.
The event made national headlines—
Caused quite a stir in the family,
Since Father ran off, hours later,
With a woman who swallowed swords,
And refused to take no for an answer.
I reveal this tidbit of information,
Merely as historical fact alone.

My sudden entrance into calamity,
Came at a costly price—
An admission ticket I've yet to cash,
If I could only gauge its worth.
That I find I'm constantly drawn
To tight quarters and little space,
Should arrive without surprise.
I'm far more comfortable in places
Where others squeal or scream—
Unsure of the destination ahead.
This, then, is cargo I carry;
Safe passage through a curious life.

THAT WAS YOU; WASN'T IT?

That was you; wasn't it?
Junior high school juvenile delinquent,
Chain smoking a pack of Kools—
Your leather collar flipped up.
You had no trouble, whatsoever,
Giving the principal the bird,
Before he called your parents,
Who didn't give a rat's ass
If you were suspended or not.
Just don't get caught, the old man sighed,
Pouring another pint of stout
To drink your poor mother away.

That was you; wasn't it?
Taking one step forward and two back,
Leaving the house at 16,
To move halfway across the country,
Where no one knew your name
Or the dreaded family curse
You swore you could not escape.
When the Navy wouldn't enlist you,
The Army said, *Step right up, Son*.
And you kept your nose clean
Until your temper got the best of you.
Dishonorable discharge, the document read.

That was you; wasn't it?
Betting your savings on a longshot
Whose maiden had not been broken,
Returning home, penniless, years later,
Thinking you were owed something, at least,

Bart Edelman

Despite your parents untimely demise.
The bank was simply an afterthought,
If all else came up empty.
And the gun's discharge was an accident—
The teller should have done as told.
But you did make the front page news.
That was you; wasn't it?

EXIT

They told us there was an exit,
Yet we could never find it—
So it became no use to us,
And we filled our young lives
With nothing but entrances,
One after another, after another.
We were always opening doors,
Wherever we went, for weeks on end,
Until we could no longer access
The constant approaches we took.
It was only in the beginning—
When we had a taste for the chase—
That we thought a challenge
Might very well do us good,
Strengthen our ability to problem solve,
Accept the practical, predictable advice.
However, it came at quite a cost—
This gradual process of discovery
And the final test teaching us
There was, simply, no way out—
Any means of escape, impossible.
Surely, we had the hard evidence
To prove it, even in a court of law—
If given half the chance—
But it never came down to this.
Without the proper outlet available,
We were forced to shelter-in-place,
Huddle together for safe keeping—
Dismiss what options remained.

Bart Edelman

IN HEAVEN

In heaven they know your work—
Catalogue every poem you've written,
Commit them to memory, forevermore.
Bradbury and you huddle together
Over a steaming cup of java,
Discussing relevant issues each morning,
Giggling until the afternoon
Releases you to destiny's retreat.
How sublime are the clouds
Buttoning up the universe below,
Telling you it's all been worth
The journey to reach this celestial home
You'll never need leave again.

Tomorrow, Twain shall come calling.
He enjoys his billiards and bourbon—
Not necessarily in that order.
Frost will soon follow next week,
Partial to easy wind and downy flake,
Arriving atop his splendid little horse.
Bob's always good for a serious chat—
No longer rushed by daily matters—
Nary a promise to keep.
It's a jolly, good life here, indeed.
You can still write, now and then,
When thoughts sneak up on you,
Like visits from long-lost friends.

AFTERNOON

RAVEN

Today, sorting laundry,
I found a dazed raven,
Half asleep in my pocket.
Poor thing appeared haggard,
Told me he hadn't enjoyed
A moment's rest in ages,
As surely seemed the case.
The bird recited metric verse—
The entire afternoon—
Claimed he was a union member,
But then it all went to snot.
He was now disenfranchised:
Out of work, out of money,
And still had hungry mouths
Left to feed in a nest,
Somewhere south of Baltimore;
It made me weep, I'll admit.
However, late for supper,
I placed him gently in the dryer,
Set the cycle to permanent press,
Wished him all the best,
Got on with my life.

PATRON SAINT

Leonard begs for a patron saint
To protect him from harm.
Sister Oona suggests Saint Sven—
One of the newer breeds—
A man who came to the Lord,
After his own personal struggles
Brought him to his knees,
Before he cut them off—
A supreme offering, if you will.
Leonard wonders, day after day,
Could he commit such a sacrifice?
Sever the appropriate body part?
Would an ear, finger, or toe suffice?
Or need he go bolder?
He knows the stakes are high.
A false, foolish move, now,
And he'll slide deeper and deeper
Into the color of despair—
For which no name exists.
Leonard contacts the Almighty,
Asks him to deliver a sign—
Some gentle declaration, at least—
One last beacon of hope?
But only silence follows.
Leonard raises the knife higher,
Lets it drop, wherever God pleases.

Bart Edelman

THE MIDWAY

I've tried to find the Midway,
Quite a few times now,
But to no avail, I'm afraid.
It simply evades me, at all costs,
Despite the map I carry
In the chest pocket of my shirt,
Directing me to the very spot
Where the hoopla should occur.

I imagine I must be half the distance
Between the place I began
And the final stop on the line,
Yet no exact measurement exists.
Oddly enough, I remain in limbo,
Going both forward and backward,
Making an appraisal of my situation
A precarious and foolish call.

If I could only reach the Midway—
With its amusements and concessions galore—
This journey would have a purpose;
I might require little more.
Perhaps, what I thought was an end,
May well be dawn's disguise.
And when the sideshow barker beckons,
I'll take a step inside.

ELEMENTS

Are what they be . . .
No more, no less.
We study their course,
Try to do the best
We can in the time
It takes the sun to set,
The wind to cease,
The snow to melt.
We could move elsewhere,
But then we'd need adjust
To other weather patterns—
Climate of such varied degrees,
We couldn't trace the stars,
Or know which trees
Shed their autumn leaves.
Still, though, we complain—
Swear an act of God
Waits patiently to betray us.
Yes, we grumble and groan
Each day and night away,
Pray for a short respite
Between now and then—
When nature's curious whim,
Returns to vex us again.

Bart Edelman

IN THE LIFE OF EARL

In the life of Earl,
No soul suffers distress,
Meeting an untimely end.
Hunger is not allowed
By any nation on earth.
The rich serve the poor—
Five seasons each year.

In the life of Earl,
No good deed goes unnoticed.
Charity is often celebrated
Through daily proclamations,
Worthy of fanfare and flair.
Money acts as a commodity
Without value, except for monks.

In the life of Earl,
Cats become dogs,
And dogs constantly meow
To their heart's content—
Morning, noon, and night.
Humor is a political party;
No opposition need apply.

CONSIDER THIS

The world is one dead letter
After another, after another,
Hidden in top secret drawers,
Signed by a conspiracy of vandals,
Unable to provide proper dates.

It's mind-boggling, a whodunit
You could take to the bank,
If you only knew the combination
Issued to you at birth,
When security was a gurgle away.

I tell you, it's a lot to fathom.
Who hasn't thought of crawling
Under the nearest bridge in sight,
Contacting the local troll and demanding,
Hey, you take over from here.

Like all senseless acts, I suppose,
I'm committing this one to a memory
I'll surely forget by tomorrow—
Puzzling as it may be—
Truth or humble consequence.

THE DEED

No mention of the deed made,
The entire family did its dance—
Over, around, and under it—
As if a prize would be awarded
To the relative who safely skirted
The issue for an additional year.
Surely, Aunt Betty ruled the roost.
Uncle Cliff came prepared with a joke.
Cousin Moe curled up beside the cat,
And Grandpa Ben decided nothing mattered,
Except his devotion to the Lions—
Despite their ten-game losing streak.
My mother and father, not to be outdone,
Played gin rummy outside on the veranda,
Drinking quite a few banana daiquiris,
And my sister, Bree, spent an hour or two
Removing all the pickles from a giant jar,
Before replacing them back again—
For some particularly unknown reason—
Being, of course, part of *her condition*.
By the time dinner was served,
Uncle Archie had already departed—
Due to a sudden case of the flu—
And Aunt Lydia realized she needed to bathe,
Come hell or high water, she said.
We consumed what there was of the turkey,
In far less than half an hour,
Escaping yet another holiday—
None the wiser, nor any more deficient.
Later, Bree fell asleep on my shoulder,
In the backseat of the car, halfway home.
Mother and Father spoke in hushed voices

But loud enough, finally, to mention,
Wasn't it great to see everyone again?
I wanted to ask about Dad's brother, Doug—
The guy who robbed the bank outside Detroit
And is stuck in some jail who knows where.
However, I knew it was probably a bad idea
And would hurt Dad more than I thought.
Yeah, fun to see the gang, I replied,
Simply leaving it at that.
Besides, I guess, if I really do want to know
More about the deed from anyone else,
Thanksgiving is only a year away.

SPACE

Ah, yes, and how to utilize it—
Take advantage of what's available,
Redefine its perimeters in such a way,
The unlimited expanse becomes you.
And this allocated place is a home
You've lived in your entire life—
No matter the city, state, or nation
You claim to pay your allegiance.

It's always a question of where and how—
Never who, what, when, or even why.
You don't choose the area's scope;
It selects you as the companion
It's long been waiting to serve.
How you inaugurate the alliance,
And where you envision its range,
Surely, shall sustain this union.

No need to establish boundaries—
Better yet, allow the sheer capacity
To flourish on its own basis;
At least, until a sign is given,
Revealing nature has taken her course,
And you're ready for the next phase.
Then, simply, accept the space
You've created around you.

EQUATION

I baked stars into the equation
And still came up short;
Something was definitely amiss.
All the signs screamed for me
To lead with my heart,
But I wasn't buying it.
What wind I threw to caution,
Blew right back in my face.
They say life's a waiting game,
So why pretend any longer.
I've been on hold forever—
A perpetual hesitant of high order.
The next time I'm proposed,
One plus one equals two,
And someone offers a wager
To prove it, I won't be foolish.
It's merely a sucker's bet, at best—
Chock-full of curious contradictions.
Next, they'll have me believing,
Two plus two equals four;
No good can come from that.
I don't need a degree in mathematics,
Verifying how silly it all seems.
I must show some initiative:
Tell the sun to take a hike,
Dance on the edge of darkness,
Tempt the devil one last time.

Bart Edelman

CAT? BAG?

The cat's out of the bag.
The bag's out of the cat.
What difference does it make?
And if you knew, for certain,
Who would truly be the wiser?
All hell's broken loose, again,
Yet no one has any idea what to do.
I imagine we'll shrug our shoulders—
Discuss the usual business—
As if nothing has taken place.
It's merely how it is here;
At least, where we call home.

But, then, I'm deathly afraid,
There's the matter of the cat—
Not to mention the inglorious bag,
And who gave birth to whom.
Kind of like the chicken/egg thing,
If you sit down, stretch a bit,
And think long and hard about it—
A pleasant way to spend the afternoon.
Still, a dilemma is a dilemma,
Regardless of the initial offering.
What appears to be a breakfast snack,
Remains another soul's dinner in disguise.
I guess it just shows to go:
Prepare an escape plan,
Whenever the possibility exists.

SOLACE

If you're searching for solace,
You won't find it here.
Try the local liquor store,
The dry cleaners on the corner,
Or the understaffed post office—
Pregnant with dead letters galore,
And holiday greeting cards.
Please, don't pay me a visit.
I'm thoroughly up to my ears,
Eyes, nose, mouth, and throat,
Digesting what woe remains.
Tell your sob stories to the priests
At the Church of the Good Shepherd;
After all, it's their holy business.
Leave me to my flatulent dog,
Ungrateful kids, and irritable wife.
I endure their constant demands—
Our dear family, such that we are.
As concerns the rest of you,
Seek peace where it resides.
Just keep your distance from me.

Bart Edelman

JOE DOE

Here's our review on case 5117115 . . .
We cannot arrive at a proper prognosis,
When the patient refuses to engage
In any therapeutic practices
Necessary in his steps towards progress.
If not addressed, almost immediately,
We must consider suspending treatment
Already administered to Mr. Joe Doe,
As he appears unwilling or unable
To know what's in his best interest.

A complete history would be beneficial;
However, Mr. Doe will not provide it,
Leaving us somewhere in the dark.
The man exhibits signs of prior trauma.
He has, obviously, been quite neglected,
But when, and by whom, remains a mystery.
Dr. Schwartz wants one last crack at him—
To see if he can make a breakthrough.
Pending that final action, though,
We simply may have to let Doe go,
For his sake, and ours, of course.

CLAMOR OF THE LAMBS

Clarice may, or may not, be hearing
The silence of the lambs, these days,
Yet I can assure you,
I still listen for any bleat
They make throughout the night.
And like her, I would save them—
If only I were able.
Nevertheless, I require my sleep,
And other dreams, even more terrifying,
Compel me to take medication,
Placing me in the deep zone—
Halfway between a heaven and hell
I am forced to imagine.

Ah, yes, but, dear, sweet Clarice . . .
What has fate prepared for her?
Is she condemned to chase criminals
Across crooked lines the FBI has drawn,
Merely to capture Public Enemy #1?
Perhaps, it would be better
If she simply returned to Montana
And made penance with the flock;
It might do wonders for her soul.
As for me, I also need a break,
Miles away from the clamor
My mind finds to spook me.
Now, the lambs are sheep—
Far too plentiful to count.

Bart Edelman

WHAT IF?

What if what you thought you saw
Had not even occurred?
As though there was a magic act—
Some sleight of hand at work—
To deem you an accomplice,
But you never remotely knew
Why the plan was devised for you.

What if they took you on a ride
In a car without wheels,
And you thought you were racing
At top speed down the boulevard;
However, you were simply asleep,
While they filmed a documentary
Where you sat, parked in neutral.

What if the orange you ate,
Suddenly became a pear, just for spite,
And you were left clutching
A bag full of green apples
You could ill afford to purchase.
Who would expect payment
On any given Sunday—
Let alone the first Monday of the month.

What if a tie went to the runner,
Yet the pitcher had something else in mind—
Say, Hey, an over-the-shoulder catch
From 425 feet straight away.
Now that would make you think twice,
Before you put yourself in position
To play the game over again.

FLAT

When I eventually came to see
The world as flat as a board,
It was such a comfort.
I found myself fully relaxed—
For the first time in my life.
Now, it all makes perfect sense.
Every question I have is answered
By this basic, undeniable fact,
Long rumored to be false.

I don't need a membership card
To any society or historical group;
It just seems beyond logical.
Folks can only go so far
Before they run out of space—
Take it to the limit, if you will,
And drop like a stone
Into the great void they deserve—
Probably for unpardonable deeds.

I've read theories up the ying-yang,
Concerning spheres, discs, and curves.
No amount of scientific data
Need rock my horizontal world.
I bear witness to what I perceive;
Give me one good reason to disbelieve.
Let gravity, or the lack of it,
Rot in its own peculiar hell.
If I keep to the straight and narrow,
My feet will always grip earth—
Descent an impossibility.

Bart Edelman

EVENING

WHERE ARE YOU, OSBALDO?

The night twists tighter—
A tourniquet of desire.
And we can't help but whisper,
Where are you, Osbaldo?
What promises have you made
Nameless hungry women,
Seated at banquet dinners
You do not expect to attend.
How long can you pinwheel
Between each flickering star,
Displaying smile after smile,
Although solitude's luxury
Confines you to impure thoughts.
One day the clever moon
Will be done with you, forever.
You'll spin out of control,
In an orbit dawn delivers
To the last available address,
Lurking beside your name.
Mismatched clothes still remain—
Waiting for you to claim—
Yet you'll never wear them again.

FUSE

Like the rest of us,
It's often inclined to trip—
Every now and then—
When the circuits overload
And the current's flow
Has nowhere else to go.
A simple fix, of course,
Demands we reset the breaker,
Or replace the broken fuse—
Might it ever come to that.

I imagine I'd be better,
If this were my only fate,
Powering off and back on, again,
At so much as a moment's notice.
Let destiny grind to a halt,
Because of a bad connection,
Hidden somewhere in the system—
Undiagnosed until I've reached
What limited charge remains.

Perhaps, I'm on a slow decline,
Losing juice without realizing it.
Should I open up, one day,
To a more thorough examination,
Who knows what an electrician may find.
For now, I'm humming along—
Rock steady and ready—
Not even a surge in mind.
Yet I sense, at any time,
I could blow sky high . . .
And burn this old house down.

Bart Edelman

IT'S A PIG, OF COURSE

It's a pig, all right;
It squeaks with delight
At its own puffy sight,
And punctures the night
With its pink brand of fright.
It's a pig, all right.

It's a pig, if you please,
Always waiting to seize
Its prey by the knees,
So filled with disease—
Stone-deaf to all pleas—
It's a pig, if you please.

It's a pig, sure enough,
Part oink and part bluff,
Inclined to be gruff
When the truth turns tough,
And it's left in the rough.
It's a pig, sure enough.

It's a pig, of course,
Not a deer or a horse.
There's no need to endorse
A creature this coarse;
Please consider the source.
Yes, it's a pig, of course.

VOICE OF AMERICA

Someone's calling my cell phone,
But I don't recognize the number.
It's probably a poor fellow,
Attempting to sell me aluminum siding
Or give me a free trip to the Bahamas
If I agree to complete a survey.
Lately, this is the extent of my affairs—
One telemarketer after the next,
Randomly guiding me through the day.
And even though we don't exchange words,
I hear the voice of America
Begging me to *buy, buy, buy, buy* . . .
Purchase everything I can possibly afford
Before the bottom drops out,
I spend my entire bankroll,
And take the last train to Hackensack.

At night, when I turn towards sleep,
I listen to the chorus of wails—
One choir, decidedly off-key,
Yet haunting in its chant, nevertheless.
I dream, non-stop, of the mercenary yawp—
A howling that threatens to displace me.
The imaginary faces crowd beside my bed,
Imploring me to come to my senses;
After all, this is the United States, God damn it!
Suddenly, I believe, for the moment,
I could use my rugs steam cleaned,
My closets and bedroom expanded,
My driveway repaved, yet again,
And my internet, phone, and TV bundled,
Keeping the voice of America
Never more than another offer away.

Bart Edelman

ON FINDING SOMEONE WHO LOVED YOU
(LOVES YOU NO MORE)

If it never needed to be said,
You simply wouldn't know.
Off you'd go to the country
And leave the city far behind.
A month's vacation would do the trick,
But that's not how you learn of love lost,
How you react to abandonment,
And what it means to survive.
Believe me, I've tried—and failed.
When presented with mere facts alone,
The obvious response is to deny
As much, and as often, as possible,
For, at least, the time it took
To cultivate what is no more.

You'll require a navy of faith—
Friends who won't take no for an answer,
And have been on the island
You inhabit in your grief.
Let them be the vessel sailing
Between you and the next day.
Never measure progress by distance;
This can lead to your undoing.
It took you an entire life
To give all you did so freely.
Now you must heal yourself
Through the sorrow grace dictates,
When the heart's song,
Longs to sing again.

WAITING

Tom Petty tells me each evening,
The waiting is the hardest part,
Yet while I must agree,
Wholeheartedly, by day's end,
I'm drained with the process—
A runaway dream my reward.

I try to come to grips—
Place everything in perspective,
Evaluate life at the present point,
But there's always loose threads
Demanding a knot somewhere,
And I feel obligated to serve
The next client in line.

If I could only find time
To spring into action mode—
Without a moment's delay—
I may short-circuit hesitation,
Plaguing what dictates fate.

However, when it matters,
I hang fire, I'm afraid—
Let nature take its course,
And there I stand, petrified,
Holding a hat in my hand,
Unwilling to place it on my head.

Bart Edelman

THE LOBSTERMAN

The lobsterman has few qualms,
Concerning the state of his life.
He knows the lethal trap
His wife has set for him—
How ironic it all seems.
Like his father before him,
And his grandfather, as well,
He's long accepted this chosen trade—
Work from which he does not shirk.

Early each morning his day begins.
He prepares the wooden pots,
Carefully maintaining them to allow
The maximum capacity possible.
As he breaks away from shore,
He sings the song he was taught:
A lobster, a lobster, a lobster,
A lobster I must be,
If not for the hope of tomorrow,
If not for the love of the sea.

Late afternoon, exhaustion arrives.
He checks the crates and hopes
There is enough of a haul
To make it worth his while.
When he finally reaches home,
She has dinner ready for him,
But is fast asleep in the bed
They share through loneliness.
He eats by silent candlelight,
Awaiting his remaining fate.

JAMES SO DEAN

Head so heavy,
Heart so bold,
Ford so Chevy,
Soul so cold.

Eyes so blue,
Feet so wide,
Giant so true,
Tongue so tied.

Smile so nice,
Voice so shy,
Once so twice,
Low so high.

Porsche so clean,
Road so slick,
James so Dean,
Death so quick.

REUNION

Neither king, nor queen.
No golden crown or silver tiara,
And no roses to speak of—
Only the ravaged photographs—
Old farts on a dance floor
We can no longer navigate—
An ancient ship of bloody fools.

We wonder what possesses us
To hold such lurid poses,
Every five years like clockwork.
If the invitations were never sent,
We would not know where to go,
And the show might mercifully close—
Before the next stroke struck.

Yet for those who do attend,
Celebration is in the air—
Outfits chosen months ahead.
We memorialize the past,
Crisscrossing wires, state to state,
Reliving history each chance we get—
Even with our last breath.

JUANITA MIRANDA MONTANA

Juanita Miranda Montana . . .
If truth be told,
I wanted to marry you
The moment we met,
Simply for your name alone—
The way it managed to roll
Pleasingly off my tongue
When first I pronounced it.

Juanita Miranda Montana . . .
I dream of beginning each day,
Asking how you passed the night,
Serving you breakfast in bed:
A scone, an orange, a coffee—
Anything to make your journey
Through this complicated world,
A breath of undeniable ease.

Juanita Miranda Montana . . .
If you were my wife,
I would never request you change
A name so filled with song,
I could sing it forever—
Trilling from season to season,
Knowing you would be listening—
Until we are no more.

Bart Edelman

METROPOLIS OF INSOMNIA

In the metropolis of insomnia,
Sleep is, obviously, not an option.
Everyone goes about their business,
Trance-like, as if awaiting trains
Destined never to arrive.
Those who stand upright,
Do so contorted against posts,
Dotting tracks that stretch as far
As the eye can see—
If only it were open
To a notion called sight.

Often, you hear the thud of unfortunates
Dropping from utter exhaustion
Upon the various platforms—
Splayed arteries in all directions.
Immediately, the secret police
Cart their lifeless bodies away
To a place where eternal rest
Provides a final solution—
Should we wish to call it so.

And who knows if the departed
Remain entombed, at all.
To ask such a question
Surely puts you on a list
No one cares to create,
Considering the current state.
Best just to be thankful
And inhale what breath
Keeps us alive and barely awake—
At least until the next day breaks
Through the night's black shell.

IF ONLY I COULD

Because you threatened me with love,
Escape became my sole exit.
And there never was a question of *if*—
Just *when* the deed could be done.
Had a freight train been available,
I would have hopped it, posthaste,
Before you were through speaking,
Imploring me to hang in there—
Give it one final chance.

Let's face it; you've always known
I was never any good at playing
This impractical game called house.
It seems to go against my nature,
For all the reasons we've discussed,
Since the red sky opened up
And dropped us in your bed—
Fateful as the ring you later gave me—
This bond I was forced to break.

You come from a long line of healers.
Saving is a grace you practice well.
But I'm past the point of redemption,
And there's no church left to attend.
Surely, you'll find another more worthy,
Who's been seeking someone like you
To provide them a stable life—
Structure and form I eschew.
All that remains is the truth:
I would love you, if only I could.

WALTER WHITE AND THE FIVE DWARFS

Sneezy died in the thick of winter;
It wasn't totally unexpected.
He'd been sick a long time
Before pneumonia struck him down—
On Christmas Eve, of all days.

Sleepy, to the contrary, was never ill
A single day in his life—
The picture of perfect health.
He just failed to wake up
One Sunday morning in May,
And was gone, lickity split.

Walter White tightroped the Grim Reaper,
Escaping rather dazed and confused,
After his existential brush with death,
Awaking near a cottage, deep in the forest—
So much for astral projection.

The remaining dwarfs worshipped Walter.
He was humorous, debonair, and urbane,
Traveling romantic places unknown to them.
Only Doc had serious concerns,
But he kept them to himself.

Dopey, Happy, Bashful, and Grumpy,
Still worked, mining for gemstones,
And hadn't a clue what Walter did,
While they were out making ends meet.
Any mention of the fair Snow was verboten.
She had run off with a tall hunter
And couldn't be bothered with small details.

Walter, though, was cooking up plans
To return to his true calling.
He created a lab in a remote shed,
Secretly storing his product for years,
Confessing only to Dopey in a pitiful moment,
When the beardless mute needed
To survive a serious case of hives.

Yes, on it went, quite swimmingly,
Until Walter got a yen for the big city—
Let's simply call it Albuquerque—
And disappeared in an unmarked van
He had disguised as a container.

The dwarfs were so deservedly depressed,
They decided to rename themselves:
Rock, Slappy, Brashful, Dumpy, and Mopey.
But it couldn't cure a hideous malaise,
And they eventually went to their graves
Without the affection each of them craved.

Sadly, they did not live happily ever after,
Although they did make quite a fortune—
High rollers in the diamond trade.

ACCIDENT, ILLNESS, RECKONING

I'm told, quite matter-of-factly,
I'm always looking for trouble.
If it's anywhere in the vicinity,
I'm bound and determined to find it—
Despite reason, prejudice or delay.
I can smell the scent of doom,
During my morning ablutions,
Throughout the day's dwindling hours,
And when night becomes dark enough
For me to play poker with my shadow—
Or any ghost who is available.

It's not as though I was raised
By warlocks, witches, wombats.
No, I assure you, steadfastly,
There was plenty of love to pass around.
Mom, Dad, and my siblings doted on me,
But I was always drawn to the macabre.
Even after a grade school chum vanished
And was found at the bottom of a lake,
I wondered about his last thoughts—
How death tasted on a summer afternoon.

I try and picture my own demise.
Whether I could ever do myself in—
Achieve the so-called unpardonable act.
Yet, also drawn to the element of surprise,
I often ponder my ultimate fate,
Without planning each detail out.
Yes, that seems to suit me fine.
Accident, illness, reckoning . . .
It's all pretty much the same, I guess—
Gets you where you need to go.

THE SONG

Once she sang the song,
Her singing never stopped.
It wafted through the streets,
Behind Marie's Pastry Shop,
Inside Pascal Renoir's Haberdashery,
Above St. Christopher's Church,
And out across the canal—
Where lovers chose to boat.
It was an unforgettable tune
You could not relinquish,
As long as you retained breath.
The simple melody and verse,
Visited when you needed
A respite from the dreary day,
Or a private interlude,
Often before drinking pastis,
Alone in a neighborhood café.
Long ago, you wisely decided,
The song should be played
At a funeral, especially yours.
The thought brings a smile,
Every time you propose it—
An overture, perhaps, to a life
You wish you lived . . . and did.

Bart Edelman

THE LAST WORD

I think of the last word—
When it will be written,
How it may possibly sound,
What the meaning shall convey.
And I wonder, perchance,
If I can measure its weight,
By the length of a feather
Yesterday's sparrow left behind,
On the path to my loft,
In the house I call home.

I ponder what time remains—
Troubling me, now and then.
Yet I know not to stop,
For fear I'll be unable
To start the process again—
Distinguish winter from spring,
Turn summer towards fall.
Just the sort of mutation
I sense could haunt me
In doubt's final moments.

Archbishop Anthony Bloom concedes,
The proper response to love
Is to accept it.
There is nothing to do.
So, too, must it follow,
This slow work I practice—
Painstaking at its every letter—
A crawl towards the light
I find in a dark corner,
Waiting to address the night.

WHISTLING TO TRICK THE WIND

THE WOODPECKER

To know the length of my shadow
Grows smaller and smaller each year,
Makes me pause in mid-thought—
Unable to complete the sentence
It seems I need serve.
I realize no escape is possible.
Fate has a way of convincing,
Even the most ardent skeptic,
We can only go so far
Before the last chip is cashed,
And we're no longer playing
With the benefit of house money.

Each night, as sleep approaches—
If I'm lucky enough to find it—
I ask myself what I've done
To earn admission into heaven.
That I often come up empty
Gives me ample cause for sorrow.
And I think the time appears short;
I must learn to do better,
Should I expect a reprieve.
When the morning mercifully arrives,
I hear my friend, the woodpecker,
Drilling patiently, outside the window.
Is his work any different than mine?

TO CLAIM THE DEAD

He knew all along
It would have to end;
She could only be driven so far.
He didn't have enough gas
In his tank for the likes of her—
Forget the water, oil, and anti-freeze.
She had already slowly begun
To apply the brakes,
Despite her pretty feet
Resting nowhere near the pedal.

He'd been foolish to think otherwise—
Believe a future existed
When they had not embraced the past,
And the present was less than promising.
He realized she wanted to go places,
Travel in circles which made him dizzy,
Shift twice and ask questions later,
Even if she stalled out along the way.
A smart man would have seen this coming,
Stayed far out of her lane,
Allowed her to pass, with caution,
But he wasn't that man—
Far from it.

What on earth would he tell his pals
After it all came crashing down?
They'd warned him from the start,
Said she was out of his league,
And he had her picture to prove it.
He knew it was pathetic;

Bart Edelman

He couldn't possibly stop—
Pull over to the side of the road,
Turn his emergency blinkers on,
Wait for the sound the ambulance made
When it came to claim the dead.

ANYONE BUT BARRYMORE

On his best day
He's anyone but Barrymore:
Unshaven, unkempt, untamed.
He hopes to meet a woman
Much like himself,
Who will not worry
About outside appearances,
A recent list of credits,
Money in the bank,
The proper Westside address.
He thinks, lately, he's been
On a particularly bad roll;
Fate has cooked the dice,
And they're not serving him well—
These long days and nights.

Perhaps, he needs to attend
The kinds of Bohemian places
Where his true creative calling
Comes more into focus,
Clean up his rough image,
Let the boyish charm
Take control of his life—
Even though he doesn't want
To sell his soul to Hollywood
And the first matrimonial agent
He meets on the granite street,
Filled with one star after another.
Still, a tall, elegant woman—
Slightly resembling Bacall—
Wouldn't be bad, at all.

Bart Edelman

ALL THE PRETTY YOUNG GIRLS

Struggle gamely with their beauty,
Fragile as pennywhistle thistles
Caught in a terrible wind,
Howling through their lives.
And what of the trouble ahead,
Disillusioned spirits seeking refuge,
Blinking out the truthful lies
No one cares to believe.
What shall become of dumb love
They hold in cold hearts,
Never to open again.
All the pretty young girls,
Choked by fate they check
At cloakrooms in restaurants—
Where they pass on dessert
And feast on sorrow.

FOOTNOTE

It's how you view yourself now—
Nothing but a reference
At the bottom of the page—
One note employed to elucidate
A specific point well taken,
Yet, perhaps, never explained enough
To keep the reader on the mark.
In your youth you imagined
You might be more than a mere comment,
Cited on an as-needed basis—
Required evidence of the lowest order.
However, it's safe to say,
Space still remains for you,
Albeit, often, south of the border—
The last tortilla on the truck,
Bound for a single destination.
And when the text of your life
Demands examination from a source
Whose credit seems beyond reproach,
Think of all you have given
To the field of scholarly discourse,
And choose the high road—
Before you slip into obscurity.

Bart Edelman

I LOVE YOU TRULY, GEORGE CLOONEY

Oh, George Clooney,
What I wouldn't do for you:
Clean you, clothe you, cook for you;
Carry your protest signs
Up and down Fifth Avenue,
Challenge every single rumor
Concerning your so-called sexuality,
As if ambiguity were a crime.

Oh, George Clooney,
If you could only come home to me
Each night in Staten Island,
We'd make beautiful music
Until the wee hours, you'd see.
I'd buy you chocolates
And an array of flowers
To christen the life we'd share.
I'd swear my devotion to you
On a stack of leather Bibles,
Stretched as high as the Empire State Building.

Oh, George Clooney,
I'll proudly play Catwoman,
If you'll remain Batman.
And you won't desire Lake Como
Once you view the little nest
I've built for us on Richmond Avenue,
One story above Al's Deli,
Where the brisket and rye
Make you tremble and sigh.

Oh, George Clooney,
You won't need to save
Another soul in the world—
Once you surrender to me.
They'll be enough peace between us
You won't have to travel the globe,
Seeking another righteous cause.
O (Sweet) *Brother, Where Art Thou?*
I love you truly, George Clooney.

THE AGE OF BELIEF

They say, on the morning news,
It's the age of belief,
But, quite frankly,
I appear faithless these days,
Checking out of my life
Every chance I get.

Perhaps, it's nothing at all,
A mere case of malaise—
Or what my friend, Fabrice,
Refers to as ennui—
This boredom of the soul
I am unable to escape.

And, yet, how convenient it would be
If I could only believe
In anything, whatsoever.
I don't need to entertain
A grand concept of God,
Or even love, for that matter;
These ideas burden the mind.

What I seek is nothing more
Than the evening breeze at my back—
Whisper of wind so free,
It never disrupts the universe.

THIN AIR

Anna sensed his uncanny ability
To grow taller and taller,
While she appeared smaller,
Shrinking by the minute—
The sweep of a second hand
Ready to do her in,
Ticking its way across her tiny face.

True, she was hardly surprised
By this wrinkle in time.
Daily she checked the mirror,
Noticing how her size
Diminished with every hour.
When he returned from work,
Each evening at eight,
She had to crane her neck so high—
Merely to glimpse him—
She often thought better of it
And crawled further away.

If he missed her at all,
He never let it be known
But kept on, splendidly,
As if they saw eye to eye.
He carried on conversations with her,
Yet she failed to understand
Anything he said;
How could she,
With his head above the clouds.
Eventually, she lost sight of him—
Unaware he was even there—
Disappearing into thin air.

Bart Edelman

KING OF THE DROPOUTS

Disengage, disengage, disengage . . .
It's all I do these days—
Post retirement, if you will.
I'm the king of the dropouts,
Releasing everything I once grasped
In the heyday, hubbub, Heisenberg,
When I couldn't race fast enough
To catch the next train to Clarksville—
No matter who was at the station,
Offering me the meteoric ride.

Now, it's always summer
In the winter of my mind.
I travel where I desire,
Free to do as I please,
Measure the morning wind—
Basic directions I chart—
With nothing more than a hat
And a pair of leather boots
To keep me upright and steady,
Even on the heels of detachment.

I no longer require a home—
Just a post office box, in case
Rare news must reach me.
As far as friends are concerned,
The fewer, the better—
At least, in this realm.
It took a lifetime and a half
For me to relinquish the past,
Lock expectations in memory drawers—
Combinations long forgotten.

MAUDE TELLS CLAUDE

Maude tells Claude it's over.
She no longer has any use for him.
Their union is a sham
She won't stand for anymore.
He can take whatever he pleases;
It's of little consequence to her.
She needs to conquer the world
Without him lollygagging around,
Complaining about this, that,
And everything under the sun.
He's turned into a *flojo*—
A lazy shadow of a man,
Living off her welfare,
Spending his entire time
Entranced by the television
And the sound of his own voice.

Maude will move to Minneapolis—
Or, possibly, Cincinnati.
Perhaps, enroll in college,
Make something of herself,
So she won't be a woman
Who never advances a step past
The man refusing to remove
An axe from her back.
Still, she must face Claude again,
Before she makes her escape,
Climb through the window
She's left slightly ajar—
Slowly place one foot
In front of the other.

Bart Edelman

I'M FINE

My brother tells me I'm pretty.
My sister tells me I'm plain.
My husband tells me I'm fine.

My mother tells me I'm thin.
My mirror tells me I'm fat.
My husband tells me I'm fine.

My friends tell me I'm smart.
My boss tells me I'm stupid.
My husband tells me I'm fine.

My doctor tells me I'm healthy.
My monthly tells me I'm sick.
My husband tells me I'm fine.

My beautician tells me I'm open.
My shrink tells me I'm closed.
My husband tells me I'm fine.

My Lexus tells me I'm rich.
My bankbook tells me I'm poor.
My husband tells me I'm fine.

My pastor tells me I'm saved.
My God tells me I'm damned.
My husband tells me I'm fine.

HAVE YOU EVER BEEN TO WICHITA?

When she asked me,
Have you ever been to Wichita?
I thought I was dead.
I might as well have carried
The dreaded doornail in my pocket—
Or a fish upon my head—
The stinkier, the better.
At least, that might have prevented me
From being so forthcoming,
Ordering a third drink,
Giving her a second glance,
Before realizing she was my first wife.

Listen, the lighting in the bar
Had to be God-awful, to say the least.
And she was, undeniably, wearing
One of her numerous wigs.
Still, I should have picked up
Any of a hundred clues:
The voice with the Brooklyn lilt,
The laugh like a jackhammer,
The eyebrows, always in mid twitch,
And the fingers, of course—
Nine digits in motion,
Counting everything in sight.

She'd told me, when I met her,
Amnesia ran in her family—
History so cruel, it could easily outrace dawn.
And, now, I firmly believed,
The malady had caught up with her.
Yet, she kept curiously watching me—

Bart Edelman

Until the time I excused myself—
Insisting I reminded her of someone familiar.
When I reached the street,
I heard her softly call after me:
Perhaps, it wasn't Wichita, at all.
Have you ever been to Des Moines?

LOST AT SEA

You waited too long this time
And knew what that meant.
Now there was no safe return,
No sanctuary in sight,
No harbor for light—
Retreat, utterly hopeless.
You heard before of men
Who wandered too far from shore
And became lost at sea,
Simply because they failed to accept
What nature offered them,
Fishing for the kind of humility
Their pride could never allow.
Yes, foolish is the pitiful love
A sailor makes to the mistress
From whom no escape remains—
Only the eternal rest he takes,
Slipping gently beneath the waves
To embrace the green grave.

Bart Edelman

THE BUSINESS OF LOVE

I should have retired
From the business of love
While I still had the chance,
But I was foolish
And far too unwise
For my own good.

I should have called it a day—
Refused the transaction—
Placed a sign upon my door,
Left the little shop
I opened before the war,
When hope remained an option.

I should have been clever—
Concealed my many motives—
Kept a few coins in my vest,
Never let anyone else know
The fear I fought each night,
Just thinking of being alone.

I should have realized
What it was I had to lose—
How solitude is only an offer
Until the final bill comes due—
Calculated all I'd need to pay
For my investment in you.

REVELATION

When my father revealed
He once murdered a man in Canada
At the age of 19,
It failed to surprise me.
He never told me the exact details—
And I never asked—
Knowing the admission was more than enough.
He was 92 and ready to call it a life.

The few times I saw him,
Before the end finally came,
He referred to it as *the incident*,
And he seemed to feel, perhaps,
My total lack of reaction
Gave him permission to mention it, again,
As if this were his dying request.

The last day I visited him,
I gathered up the courage to question
Whether my mother knew
About the so-called *incident*,
At any time before she passed away,
But he simply muttered, *Never*,
Paused for a moment,
And then said, matter-of-factly,
I'd rather kill myself,
Than admit such a thing to her.

After my father's death—
For the first time since I was a small boy—
I began to wish I were not an only child,

Bart Edelman

Remembering how lonely I felt
On certain weekday afternoons—
In the white heat of summer—
When the weight of tomorrow
Had not yet arrived at my front door.

COASTAL LAGOON

I am unsure of lust,
Residing in curious places
Where I would never suspect:
The eye of a tree,
The belly of a rock,
The toe of a cloud.

I do not presume to know
How to find desire
Around the jolly corner,
Over the next bluff,
Under the back steps.

I become somewhat flustered—
All too often, I'm afraid—
When I pretend passion
Thinks on its feet,
Sings for its supper,
Dreams of its demise.

But I have, most recently,
Witnessed the afterglow
Love casts across the floor
On a candlelit night,
In a circular room,
Beside a coastal lagoon.

Bart Edelman

GO GENTLE INTO THAT GOOD NIGHT

Please, please, go gentle into that good night,
Old age should never burn at close of day;
And do not rage against the dying light.

Wise women at their end know death is right,
Because their words leave little left to say;
Please, please, go gentle into that good night.

Good women watch each wave and see how bright
Their deeds have danced across a silver bay,
And do not rage against the dying light.

Wild women catch and sing the sun in flight,
They learn to let grief hurry on its way,
Please, please, go gentle into that good night.

Brave women, near the last, adjust their sight
Through eyes that search to find a final ray,
They do not rage against the dying light.

And you, my mother, climb the lofty height,
Bless every step you calmly take, I pray.
Please, please, go gentle into that good night.
And do not rage against the dying light.

—after Dylan Thomas

HOW I CAME TO YOU

Bankrupt . . . petty . . . poor . . .
Without a drop of honey
Coursing through my veins,
The ire from another life
I led in slow motion,
When my soul departed
The moment I turned away
To scowl at the stars.

Aimless . . . shiftless . . . stuck . . .
In nothing except the mire
I could not escape,
But grew to embrace,
Because once you wear
The cloak of loneliness—
Day in and day out—
You don't know how else to dress.

Admit . . . permit . . . submit . . .
Vows I refused to keep
Until I came to you
And heard you reveal them
For the first time—
This gift, a blessing,
To free me from myself.

WHISTLING TO TRICK THE WIND

Ran out of words—
One letter at a time—
Found no use for them.
Spoke in speechless sounds
Only the deaf can hear.

Lost his job,
Refused to repeat destinations
The train passed as it wound its way
From the mouth of Manhattan
Through the belly of Brooklyn.

Gave his friends the heave-ho,
When they requested an intervention,
Paid the neighbors for their services,
Climbed up the roof in the dark
And communed with the moon.

Came to believe in a God
Whose perfection was never in question,
Promised to wire his mouth shut
If the Almighty would agree
To keep his miracles to himself.

Lived a rather fruitful life
In the company of boulders—
Too old and tired to converse—
Took his final act of contrition,
Whistling to trick the wind.

THE GEOGRAPHER'S WIFE

THE GEOGRAPHER'S WIFE

Pity the poor geographer's wife,
Who spends most of her life
Missing him in every isthmus,
Desert, mountain, valley,
He's had the pleasure to explore.
He claims it's not his fault.
The field takes him away,
Draws him east, west, north, and south
At a moment's notice—
Often in the middle of the night
While she rises from their tiny bed,
And he packs a bag of silence
Only a secret can keep.

He swears she knew about his desire—
The longing to touch air, land, sea—
This need to leave a piece of himself
Wherever he can, survey
The climatic conditions of an earth so vast
He can barely comprehend it all.
When she timidly asks,
Upon each of his returns,
How it is they cannot travel together—
Why he will not share his life's work—
He struggles so with his words,
She retreats to her ball of yarn
To darn yet another sock,
Steady herself for the week
They have before his next departure.

Ah, yes, pity the poor geographer's wife,
Who watches the house grow
More and more around her every day.

THE CONTIGUOUS 48

Before Uncle Irv died,
He said he wanted to spend the night
In every state in the Union—
At least the contiguous 48.
He didn't seem to care
For Alaska or Hawaii,
Let alone Puerto Rico
And the other off-shore U.S. territories—
Something about separation—
The notion that the nation
Should not suffer from marginalization,
To one degree or another.

We all thought it had to do
With Irv's own station in life,
Or lack of it, for that matter.
He always had a problem
Finding himself, more or less,
So his decision, much later in life,
To strike out on his own
In an old Ford Econoline van—
Leave us all behind—
Came as no shock or surprise.

Irv sent us a postcard each morning,
When he awoke in a different state,
And always claimed, should he ever return,
This is exactly where he wished *to expire*—
A term that found its way
Into much of his later correspondence.
We kept a fairly large map

On a wall in the basement
Of our home in Teaneck,
Would X out each state
With a red Magic Marker,
Where Irv last laid his tired head.

Alas though, when it came to pass,
Dear Uncle Irv eventually came up
Just a wee bit short of his goal.
He managed to hit 47 of the 48—
A phenomenal average in any sport—
Especially baseball, a game he truly loved.
Luckily, Irv was never aware of his failure.
He expired in a motel room,
Somewhere east of Rock Springs, Wyoming,
Passing his final, glorious moments in the sheets,
Peacefully asleep between two hookers from Casper,
Who took his wallet, his keys,
And his van, for good measure.
Knowing Uncle Irv, he would have thought
This only right and proper,
Since he had no use whatsoever,
For any worldly goods, at this point.

RAGGEDY ANN

Sued her parents last week in a Manhattan courtroom
For contributing to the delinquency of a minor,
Not providing an erstwhile education,
As well as a new Chevy pickup.

Has no friends to speak of,
Except that charlatan Barbie,
Who will not hang out with her again
After that drug-related incident;
Gee, can't a girl have fun?

Sits in her plush bedroom
Mumbling gibberish all day,
Trying to develop a language
Composed of nothing but vowels.

Wishes she could meet
A handsome boy called Andy,
So they might form a perfect union,
Dispel the swirl of countless rumors.

Thinks she should select
Another shade of hair color,
Rather than that hideous routine red
To brighten a rather dreary life
And rid herself of the past.

Pledges to change her meager name
To Irma, Gertrude, Bertha, or Dee—
Anything that has a taste of pizzazz!
Curse the little children who worship her;
Let them eat cake, or, better yet, mud pie.

Lights up a second pack of Camels for the day,
Deeming herself rough and ready
To trade in her striped leggings
For a black leather miniskirt
And a midnight blue beret.

FOREVER SPINNING

This year, boys of summer
Spring into action a few weeks early
Before the competition begins.
They gather at the ballpark,
Focus on rudimentary drills—
The skills that win championships
In Pony Leagues across America.
For hours on end, by the thousands,
Players hit fungoes to each other
Until the sun sinks lower and lower
Over the municipal park diamond.

Here are the lucky kids whose parents
Do not possess the money
To send them for eight weeks to camp,
So they spend July and August
Tethered together, honing techniques
Of bat and glove, eye and speed—
This fundamental need to elevate the team
One step closer to the success
They seek before September
Drags them back to school
And the labor each textbook provides.

But here on their home field—
Littered by the refuse of time,
The grime of soiled bases,
Imaginary foul lines—
These young sons of policemen,
Bartenders, carpenters, salesmen, cooks,
Teachers, painters, librarians, plumbers,

Bart Edelman

Assemble for one more season—
A final chance to let the game survive
Inning after golden inning,
The ball forever spinning
Through the seams of their lives.

FIRST KISS

She's got a great engine
And a real sweet chassis,
Cal says, stroking his new Dodge.
He's spent every penny he saved
For at least the last three years
On this tasty little truck,
Wishing I'd admire it,
Just the same as he does.
I chime in and tell him
It's really the cat's meow,
A one of a kind prize
He stole for half its worth.
But I feel like crap
'Cause what I'm staring at today,
Yesterday, and the past few months
Is his sister, Veronica.
Somehow, he's convinced her
To wash the truck with him,
And she's bending over
In these tight white shorts,
Cleaning the wheel covers—
Dark hair cascading down her back—
And it's getting to me, big time.

Not only is she his younger sister,
But she's my next-door neighbor, for God's sake.
He'd murder me if he knew
The track my mind is taking.
What kind of low-life guy
Lusts after his best friend's sister?
And I'm sure I'd be able
To handle it much better,

Bart Edelman

If she didn't give me
A diet of these sideways glances,
As though she somehow knows
Exactly what I'm thinking.

Wanna take her out for a spin?
Cal offers, flipping me the keys.
I gotta get ready for work,
But you're free to test her out
When Ronnie gets done hosin' her down.
Just be careful with first gear.
She sticks a bit some time.
It's all that's out of sync with her.
She just needs breakin' in.
Cal turns and walks toward the house,
Disappearing into twilight's last trance.
He doesn't see me shudder
In my ragtag leather boots.
I catch a hint of Veronica's smile,
While she peeks out at me
From below the chrome bumper.
I know my life is about to change.
I can feel it in the way
My pulse jumpstarts my heart.
And then there is nothing
But open road before us—
The taste of that first kiss.

THE WRONG SIDE OF TOMORROW

Each morning we wake up
On the wrong side of tomorrow—
Fresh tracks from the evening
Running down the length of our backs.
We say today will be different;
We adjust our engineer's caps,
Climb aboard the locomotive
We've ridden through life—
This long train of spite
We drive deep into night.
We try to obey the traffic signs
Standing between our destinations,
But there are far too many
To yield the right of way—
One cautionary tale after the other,
Far as the eye can see.
And, still, this never-ending line
Provides the only comfort we know:
The hum of each rail beneath us,
The glow of the engine's fire,
The steady tick of the brakeman's watch—
As if we could safely measure the future,
By the time it takes to arrive.

Bart Edelman

GIRLS LIKE LINKA

Girls like Linka
Pin their hair to the wind—
Ten strands at a time—
When the first sign of trouble
Threatens to overtake them.

Girls like Linka
Dream of nothing but boys
Who know how to cruise
Up and down the cruel avenues,
Littering their lives.

Girls like Linka
Behave badly at parties
Their mothers make them attend,
If only to raise suspicion,
So they will not be invited again.

Girls like Linka
Turn away from their fathers
At that time of month,
Wishing the moon was a stranger
With a spare cigarette.

Girls like Linka
Love no one but themselves—
Always dressed in black—
Each day a service,
Every night a funeral.

COLONEL SANDERS (AND THE GOSPEL OF LOVE)

Colonel Sanders speaks of love,
But, alas, no one will listen.
He's close to 120 years old
And knows he may ultimately be knocking
On the door to chicken fried heaven;
Therefore, he needs to preach
And reach each available ear,
This side east of the Mississippi.
The Good Lord saved him thirty years ago—
Delivered his God-fearing soul
From acute leukemia and pneumonia
In December of 1980—
Allowed his spirit to be reborn,
Spread salvation's sweet secret
To man, woman, and child;
However, they all appear deaf,
Unable to hear word one.

Every evening, approaching midnight,
Harlan visits a different franchise,
Lays his wrinkled, veined hands
Over the breast, legs, thighs, and wings
Of the poultry he believes
Will carry hope's eternal message
Through the sacred channels of digestion.
He massages the dear, severed birds
Long into the early morning hours,
Before he leaves to tackle the day's toil,
Witnessing on street corners in the New South—
Unrecognizable without the white suit,
Mustache and goatee he gave up three decades ago,
When he discovered light so divine,

He need not dress for dinner again.
Yet there's much work ahead . . .
The Colonel prays, in his final days,
To find the strength to continue revealing
How the power of goodness and grace
Always fills up the empty space
Between God, chicken, and man.

THE DAILY NEWS

I'm watching my weight,
Holding my tongue,
Catching my breath.

I'm hoping for love,
Waiting for fate,
Stalling for time.

I'm drawn to the chase,
Quick to the hoop,
Hip to the scene.

I'm hanging by fire,
Driving by fear,
Waking by night.

I'm playing through pain,
Jangling through June,
Soaring through space.

I'm high on speed,
Low on fuel,
Stuck on you.

Bart Edelman

WEST OF THE MISSISSIPPI

These days we're always
West of the Mississippi,
One state away from tomorrow—
The only remaining small town—
Unidentifiable on a stranger's map.
We've packed our bags so many times
It now appears useless
To have any destination in mind;
Better to drift towards eternity
With nothing but itinerant wind.

Often, we allow the river
To dictate our slow progress,
Skirting the steep sweep of banks,
Swelling when the water
Crests up to meet them,
Testing tide after tide,
Dropping the curious leadline
The dead leave behind.

No longer do we find our fate
In the promise of the frontier,
Far too late to investigate
Anything further than the taut truth,
Whose limitless boundaries border
These simple steps we take,
Making a life for ourselves—
The bifurcation of all we know:
Come north, south, east, west.

HIBERNATION

You have to think it's simply
A matter of hibernation—
Perhaps, the longest on record,
But nothing more than that.
The odds must slowly
Slide in our favor—
Over 100 seasons waiting
For just the right year
To end this drought,
Throw back our big shoulders.

The best and the brightest
Ever to play the game
Came here to the Friendly Confines
To wave the hickory stick,
Pitch fastballs of fire,
Unleash the bleachers' desire
For that last bottle of Bud,
Prior to Harry's sweet call
To take us out to the ball game.

Who really knows?
Maybe it was the curse of the goat
Or too much illumination,
Instead of the natural light arriving
Before the end of sleep,
And the eternal promise
October offers this windy city,
In exchange for another home run
Flying high above the ivy-filled wall,
With no return in sight.

Bart Edelman

Surely, Ernie would still love to play two,
If given half the chance
To tinker forever in a Cubbies uniform.
Billy, Fergie, Gabby, Kenny, Ron, and Ryne
Only need wake from slumber's embrace,
Set the record straight,
Run the table, wire to wire,
As if 1908 were yesterday,
And we could hear
The bear roar once more.

SEX ME

I want you to sex me.
She was a 19-year-old student
Who had recently taken my final exam
At the university where I taught.
There was a wild party
Inside the faculty club in Ibadan,
The week before I returned to Los Angeles.
We were all dancing the highlife—
Expatriates everywhere in sight.
The evening soon would be morning,
But her glistening skin always remained
The rich color of night.

I want you to sex me.
We stood on a balcony,
Surrounded by palm fronds,
Trying to escape the summer heat,
While the music's rapid beat
Enveloped us in a tight fist.
She was the daughter of a diplomat—
This much I certainly knew.
When she called me by my first name,
I heard the sky crack
And the wind moan;
I told her she should be going home.

I want you to sex me.
She took hold of my hand,
Placing it upon her hip,
Drawing me further into the circle
She formed for the two of us.
I did not refuse the meeting,

Bart Edelman

Until a very burly man came
To hustle the poor girl away.
He told me I was in danger
And left me with nothing more
Than her shadow's afterglow.

TE7-6330

You could dial it now—
Just for fun, of course.
Hear who would answer
On the other end.
Explain to them, in detail,
How this was your first phone number—
Complete with the Teaneck exchange—
A lifeline, so to speak,
Your link to civilization
At such a tender age.

Here is the earliest of mantras;
Please repeat after me,
In case of emergency,
TE7-6330 . . . TE7-6330 . . . TE7-6330.
And remember to enunciate clearly;
After all, this could certainly be
A matter of life and death.

Since that time, decades ago,
You've had dozens of phone numbers
In large and small states,
Stretched across the country
To indicate your exact location—
This digital form of identification
You claim without hesitation.

But that yellow phone in the kitchen
Of the house on Warren Parkway
Never seems to disappear entirely.
And you often find, even now,

Bart Edelman

Whether you're east of Eden,
South of the border,
West of the Rockies,
Or north of the Mason-Dixon line,
When someone asks how they can reach you,
You don't hesitate to respond:
TE7-6330 . . . TE7-6330 . . . TE7-6330 . . .

DESPAIR

I am done with despair—
Decided to cross it off
The extensive list of things
I need to accomplish today.
I have lived too long
In the center of its grip,
Always hoping my tall shadow
Would save the small part of me
I deemed worthy of salvation.
Now I turn away its yoke,
Even joke about the black dog—
And its habitual bark—
Who once chased me down
Desolation's dark alley—
Two short blocks from the house
I built, brick by brick.
Let another poor soul wallow,
Like a lovesick calf,
Night after captive night—
Merely for the sake of it;
Perhaps, it will do him good.
But I have a plane to catch,
A train to board,
A ship to sail,
As I patiently await
The hour of embarkation—
My left leg steady as a rail,
My right hand, open and ready,
To welcome aboard the next passenger.

Bart Edelman

SEAMSTRESSES

It tears at the fabric—
Ritual love we repair—
So seamless in its pattern,
So fickle in its spite.
We work through silence,
One thimble at a time,
Guile's long golden needles
Pointing straight towards the sky.
I thread, you mend;
You loop, I rend.
We no longer pretend
We know what reparations are due.
And yet we stitch on,
One season after another,
Each new design a landscape
Unfettered by useless measure—
This simple act of desire
We weave into the clothes we wear.

LOVE IS A LUMBERJACK WITH WINGS

Love is a lumberjack with wings,
Flying so high above your head
You fail to notice anything
Out of the ordinary,
Until it's too late,
And the saw softly falls
Squarely between your shoulders—
So much for *Have a nice day.*

Love is an acrobat on speed,
Unconcerned about a misstep here
Or a mishap there;
What's a limber body for, anyway?
Why not alter the routine
You practice on the balance beam?
And should you break a leg—
Take two and call me in the morning.

Love is a banker in denial,
Never willing to smile
At the almighty dollar sign
Flashing before his eyes,
Or the Traveler's Checks
He swears he can do without
When he enters no man's land—
Unaware of the legal tender.

Bart Edelman

FRAME BY FRAME

You're Laura Linney,
Trapped in a phone booth,
Calico cat on your head.

I'm Joe Biden,
Flubbing one more joke
By the side of the campaign trail.

We're a comical pair,
Preparing to meet our Maker
Where X marks the spot.

I sense the camera's angle,
A boom dangles overhead;
How many *T*'s are there in trouble?

You watch this futile dance,
Popcorned to the screen,
Dirty martini in hand.

We turn down the sound,
Crawl into our Hollywood bed,
Relight what's left of the night.

RETIREMENT

Sat on the shelf
In a curious corner
Of an odd room
I left long ago,
When I didn't presume
I'd ever need claim it,
But could just as easily
Allow it to rest
In the remote place
I thought was shelter.

Who could approach it then?
When the dreaded sound
Of the tick tock in its belly
Wound down each day,
As if the next hour doomed
The enormous clock I wore
Strapped to my chest
For the world to see.

Now I find I envy
The life of a hobo,
Whose toes keep him
Forever on the go,
Following only the row
Of track after track,
A straight line set
Against the distant horizon
And the stink eye of time.

Bart Edelman

I READ MY MOTHER TO SLEEP

Almost three years
Removed from my mother's death,
I study the list of books
She sent at my request,
Six months earlier,
When she was still able to write,
And her mind remained open,
Free of the disease whose claim
She could not escape.

Mother laughed when I asked
For her personal recommendations—
Avid reader that she was—
And told me in short order
She would jot down her favorites.
Somehow, she seemed surprised
I would value what books
Impacted the long life she led—
Made her the woman I admired.

Now, lucky man that I am,
With the pasture of time
Freshly spread before me,
And this semester's sabbatical
A sure thing, even in an awkward age,
I turn the page containing
The secret works my mother chose—
Those that surely sustained her
In her hour of need.

How curious then is my find:
Here's Trollope, Williams, and Graham,

Hegi, Mitchard, and Hailey—
Authors who transport me
From the end of an ocean
To small stones from a river.
Tonight, let the journey begin . . .
I read my mother to sleep.

Bart Edelman

THE LAST MOJITO

MY SONG

I intend to reach home
The day after tomorrow.
It's been a long spell.
My work, now complete,
I can finally think
Of loving you again.

You find it curious,
Perhaps, even alarming;
This compartmental process
By which I live.
You say it's something I choose,
But the nature of the job—
The sheer grind and toil . . .
Well, we've gone over this
Too often to believe
We might reconsider our positions.

And each time I leave
I know there's the chance
You won't decide to stay.
I'll return to an empty house,
Recalling the small things
Reminding me of you,
As I bump tediously
Across this unforgiving road.

Somewhere, in September's night,
I hear the sound of crickets,
Imagining the lamentation
They must feel to carry on

With all that constant clicking
And chirping to keep them company.
Would you love me any more
If that were my song?

LITTLE DADDY'S THANKSGIVING

Little Daddy flies to Iraq
To spend two and a half hours
With the unsung, beleaguered troops,
Serving them turkey and yams
On this bright Thanksgiving Day.
He poses for pictures galore
And is as kind, generous, and gracious
As he can possibly be.
After all, there is much at stake—
The war is on, for Chrissakes!
A few hours later, in Crawford, Texas,
Both Big Daddy and Barbara
Push black-eyed peas back and forth,
Awaiting their humble pumpkin pie,
And Little Daddy's triumphant return,
Eager to hear tall tales,
Resounding with redemption
And the promise of honor,
Restoring their good names
In these inhospitable times.
Meanwhile, as Air Force One
Streaks across the night sky,
Little Daddy sleeps ever so deeply,
Tuckered out from his afternoon's work
And the tryptophan shooting
Through his executive veins,
Like a lovesick missile.

ENOUGH

Knocking back Myers and Coke
On the porch at Dixie's Tavern,
Perched above the Elizabeth River
In Norfolk with Katy,
While white stars whisper:
Virginia really is for lovers.
The drive from New Jersey
Is now far behind us
And we have, rather reluctantly,
At the untimely outset,
Entered new territory to decide
If any future exists for us,
Or whether it is prudent
To let the past pull us under
And just be done with it.
But here in the evening breeze
Late June lavishes on Tidewater,
There is a hint of the summers
We left so long ago,
When we did not know
How marriage grinds us down,
Relieving us of promises
We vowed always to keep.
In Katy's eyes tonight
I see a familiar glow,
Slowly making me think
It is still possible—
The light remains lit;
Perhaps, only a flint of love
Flashes in the itinerant air . . .
And, yet, it seems enough.

Bart Edelman

POETRY EDITORS

We rock back and forth in our chairs,
Praying for anything at all
But the lingering submissions
Hovering above our heads,
Covering our small desks,
Begging each day to be read.

Here is one from a woman
Who lives on a farm in Ohio
And claims to adore turnips.
Her latest full-length manuscript
Is a series of *elegant* sonnets,
Commemorating the misbegotten root
In its magnificent glory.
Might we care to indulge
And publish at least a few gems
With which she is willing to part.

A gentleman in the throes
Of a rather nasty divorce
Has sent us his poetry—
This long litany of complaints
Concerning his shrewish wife, Claire,
Who has stolen his car,
Quit her job at the Winn-Dixie
And left town with the local pastor.
He informs us, matter-of-factly,
Should we choose to reject his work,
He may very well move to Peru.

Late at night, we picture
Sad faces and hear tearful pleas,

Before we close our eyes to sleep.
In nets of recurring dreams
We lead the July 4th parade
Down Main Street in Anytown,
Pushing rust-colored wheelbarrows,
Containing assorted pages
Spilling out from their sides,
Fluttering so high in the wind
We can not catch them all.

Bart Edelman

BED AND BRIMSTONE

The tussle of love
Knuckles between us,
Red sheets askew
Before blue fire
Burns the bed black.
By next morning
Only powdered ash remains
And white heat that hovers
Above our prickly pink skin.
Now we know how easily
Desire consumes souls
We were saving for God,
Long before it became time
To find an acre of Paradise
In the only garden named Eden.
Here is where we return
To learn apocryphal lessons
Lust has in mind for us,
When it slithers through the grass
On its empty belly.
Yet, for the moment,
Our only worry is simply
The replacement of this bed
And the sheer cost involved
To clean up residue,
Ridding the room of smoke—
The smell of brimstone
We are unable to escape.

MR. ROTUNDO

Mr. Rotundo believes
Every meal is his last—
Every drink a final drop—
That he can't get enough
Of a good thing,
And even if he could,
It would taste better
With just another serving.

Mr. Rotundo refuses
To save as much as a dime.
He lives in a tiny place
On the edge of Cemetery Park,
And drives an old car
Which barely makes it home
From the loading dock
Where he works each night.

Mr. Rotundo dreams
Of a day when all men
Will not be judged
By the color of their skin,
But by something more meaningful;
A grander fate, perhaps,
The promise of prayer—
And the perfect pastrami sandwich.

Mr. Rotundo loves
To look in the mirror
And measure his worth
By the size of his girth,

Bart Edelman

Slowly rolling his large hands
Across the wide expanse,
Kneading the soft flesh
No one else will touch.

BUFFALO DREAMS

I leave my window open
To hear the wounded buffalo
Who cannot be contained,
Forever banished by edict
From the range of the Great Plains.

The bellows arrive after midnight,
When I'm settled in snugly,
But I rise out of bed
And welcome the beast
I pray to each night.

Slowly, with cautious steps,
The huge creature appears,
Bathed in his own shadow
And the glow moonlight casts
Under a halo of stars.

In my backyard he stops
To munch the tufts of grass
And lay his burden at my feet—
The journey fraught with exhaustion,
He falls into listless sleep.

Gentle and wise is the buffalo.
Weak and wicked are the men
Foolish enough to condemn him
To wander the native land
Where America dreams no more.

Bart Edelman

PUB CRAWL

It's what we call
A night on the town—
Just the four of us:
Jensen, Brewster, Beckett, and me.
We usually end up drinking
Until one of us drops.
We're pretty evenly matched,
So we can never really tell
Who'll hit the deck first.

We've been doing this forever;
Even our wives don't seem to mind,
As long as we stick together
And keep it to ourselves.
We ought to have a designated driver,
But usually there's one of us
Who feels better than the rest,
And he takes everyone's keys,
Drives us all back home,
Picking us up in the morning
To fetch our stranded cars.

Generally, we start out at Gus's,
Then make the big loop.
Before the evening's out we'll hit
Rocky's, The Great Whale, The Runway,
Thin Lynn's, Stinky's and the 35er—
All, thank the good lord,
Within walking distance of each other.

Jensen's a scotch fanatic;
The older, the better, he claims.

Brewster tanks up on gin;
Mix 'em as high and dry
As the glint in my eye.
Beckett's never met a beer
He couldn't curl around and kiss.
And I'm partial to vodka,
Whatever you mix it with,
As long as it's not cranberry juice.

I often wonder how long
We can continue at this pace,
Having waved grace goodbye
Many summers ago.
But Beckett phoned last hour,
Declaring all the boys are up
For another night on the town,
And since we've been given permission,
We'd be utterly foolish
Not to make the crawl again.

Bart Edelman

THE DEAD RISE TWICE

In the cool grip of night—
When the dead rise twice—
I pay a visit to you,
Wearing a black rose
Pinned to my skinny lapel.
I have come for nothing
More than a hint of recognition;
A casual glance will do,
A furtive stare, far better.
I know you wonder, of course,
If this truly must be me
Returning to haunt you,
Or just some gaunt stranger
Hired for such an occasion.
And I don't necessarily have
A wishbone to pick with you,
Words which were left unsaid,
Love dissolved between us.
Tonight, I only bring you
The measure of a man departed,
A figure who slowly emerges
From the ground where you walk,
So you might glimpse
The length of my shadow
Once more before you sleep.

THE DOG

The dog is not your friend;
Kindly refuse to be misled
By the plaintive yips
And the winsome yaps
You've grown to love
Over the treacherous years
They've hoodwinked you
Into believing a pack of lies.

When it comes down to it,
Man's *best friend* is a mongrel—
A brutal, sadistic beast,
A four-legged domestic fiend;
Worse yet, of course,
For the dog is not quite
What he appears to be,
Despite the supposed centuries
Of home-grown civility.

Beware the proffered paw
And the wagging tail;
Mind the obsequious way
He follows you room to room,
But never confuse this with loyalty
Or the royalty of a true breed—
Unafraid to live alone.

Better to stick with the snake
And know from day one,
What you see and hear
Is what you get—

Bart Edelman

No false attempts to allow
A leash to be slipped
Around the serpent's neck
He was blissfully born without.

LULLABY

You've made an offer
I can't easily refuse,
But by this time of night—
Bedraggled and confused—
I know well enough
To turn away from you,
Think things through,
And see if you're still here
When the morning unravels,
Like the spool of thread
I always find in my pocket
After an evening with you.

How is it now we appear
Destined for cruel love
No one wishes upon a star,
This black celestial light—
An untimely beam, it seems,
We can never escape.
And it throws me to think
I try to solve a problem
Where no answer exists.
In due time, perchance,
We may become estranged;
My cradle shall rock,
Your bough will break.

Bart Edelman

TROUBLE

Everything pointed to trouble;
Danger and distress pranced
Topless on my wooden roof.
Misfortune grew in the garden
I tended day and night.
I was afflicted by the urge
To do myself in,
But I was so out of it
I failed to plan ahead.
I eased into my hardship
Like a pair of black loafers,
Suddenly two sizes too small.
Soon I began to pity
My big, fat, flat feet.
Woe became my middle name,
I suffered from the heebie-jeebies,
And Saint Vitus left the order
When he saw me dance;
Alas, it wasn't a pretty picture.
I found my meager little life
Lost any sense of decency.
I could smell disaster in the wind—
Hot air breathing down my back.
In other words . . .
I was hopelessly unable
To shoulder the burden I bore.
Then I simply gave up,
Drove to the hardware store,
Bought a gallon of Dutch Boy #157,
And painted myself into a corner,
Where I now live, rather comfortably,

Monopolizing every moment
I choose to spend with myself;
No more a victim of boredom—
A teller of tall tales.

Bart Edelman

FOREVER KATZ

Always Katz,
In that cold water flat
With you wearing your hat.

Constantly Katz,
Out under the stars
In my beat-up old car.

Ceaselessly Katz,
On the bright red floor
Of the Goodwill store.

Endlessly Katz,
While we are both high,
Sweet glint in your eye.

Perpetually Katz,
Where we lazily float
Half asleep in our boat.

Eternally Katz,
Right there on the stairs
After we've said our prayers.

Forever Katz,
In our soft white bed
Until we are dead.

COAT OF SORROW

And rage remains incomplete
In the beds where we sleep
Week after week, unable
To keep the pace
Of life steady, the dream
Alive and ready for what peril
Faces a nation in grief,
Impotent to speak its peace,
Except in whispered words,
Seeking to explain how rubble
And twisted steel weaken
The faith we swore to follow.

We walk the crooked streets
Through this arrhythmic city,
Watchful of a sky
Whose clouds billow and swell—
Ominous towers of smoke
Stacked high to blow us
From here to kingdom come
At a moment's notice,
Until we turn our backs,
Beating a slow retreat home
To visit empty rooms
Where yesterday's clothes hung,
Long before they vanished
And left us wearing nothing
But a coat of sorrow.

Bart Edelman

THE ROWDY BOYS

Party on and on and on,
Until the clocks run down
And the sand spills over
The twelve hands of time.
They make no plans for futures,
Ripe with nothing but renown—
Ageless sages who know
Never to stop at any town
Closing before dawn.
One by one they drink
The tumescent nights away,
Telling stories to quench
The thirst they attempt to slake
Throughout their restless lives.
And what of the girls—
Stuck in their leather boots—
Gazing longingly at rakish faces
In a circle around them.
Will they soon recover
From such secret lovers
And that first taste of spring . . .
The name of each rowdy boy
Forever engraved like a stamp
On their sweet young tongues.

HAD YOU NOT

Had you not hinted
It would be appropriate
For me to kiss you
Beneath the silver moon,
I may have avoided you
And Prufrocked myself through life—
Singing nothing but an etherized song.

Had you not suggested
Spring was a good season
For us to make love,
I might have buried myself
In a library trying to find why
Henry James' delicate wound
Kept him on the sidelines,
While the match played out
Before his fearful eyes.

Had you not intimated
I had but precious time—
And so little of that—
Until you would leave
And extinguish the sun,
I could have held
Lady Macbeth by the waist,
Waltzing her off
To the province of hell.

Had you not proposed
This compact between us,
By which we choose our words

Bart Edelman

To write the only story
Worth telling at all,
I would have closed my Bible
And nailed myself to the wall.

THE POTATO

Oh, just picture him—
Surely you must—
Lonelier than lonely still;
Sleeping in rotten fields
With not as much as a friend
To ease his vegetable plight,
Such blight you've never known
In your animal life.
And yet, there he grows,
Edible tuber that he is—
Mighty member of the nightshade clan—
So willing and utterly giving
To offer himself to your table
At even the slightest notice,
Exacting no greater payment
Than your tender hands upon his skin,
A twinkle in your eyes
For what he has endured,
And the promising future
He sacrifices to spend
This exquisite moment with you.

Bart Edelman

I KILLED THE POET

I killed the poet
For that one line,
Got him drunk on scotch
And threw him headfirst
Off the rickety bridge
Spanning the Passaic.
I watched him hit water,
Disappearing in the drink,
Never to write a word again.
I stole the sacred text
And tucked it in a pocket,
Diverted my eyes to the ground,
Beating it back home.
My trip stretched nine miles
Through twisted backroads,
Before I felt safe enough
To enter my house
And slip between walls,
Covered with the scrolls
I cleverly learned to scrawl;
Each stanza lifted
From the current of dead poets,
Asleep in their river beds
With no one to thank but me.

THE LAST MOJITO

Father Chris agrees to meet me
In the bar at the Austin Four Seasons
To discuss the state of the union.
He's unsure what he should order
And thinks a man of the cloth
Might want to stick to something
Like scotch or brandy or sherry—
Nothing too daring these days.
I'm confessing my most recent sin to him
When Lou Diamond Phillips strolls in
And plops down at our table.
He gives Father Chris the once-over,
Lamenting his perplexing career—
How he can never get away
From playing Richie Valens,
No matter what he tries to do.
The poor guy's mired in pity,
So we buy him a drink
And just kick back and listen.
As Lou's relating his story
He keeps craning his neck—
This way and that—
Until he spots a tall, gaunt fellow
Who slowly makes his way towards us,
Gives Lou a rather loud high-five,
And pulls up another chair.
Daniel Day-Lewis appears older
Than I ever remember him.
Within no more than a minute
He's telling Father Chris his tale.
He's sick of cobbling shoes

In some small town in Italy—
Why he's longing to return
To the screen he once adored,
And he's quite adamant about it.
Soon, both Lou and Dan are busy
Vying for Father Chris's attention,
While he attempts to appease
The two actors between us,
But it's very easy to sense
Even he seems a bit overwhelmed.
That's when I calmly declare
A round of mojitos might be in order.
Lou smiles and nods in agreement,
Dan holds his thumb cocked upright,
And Father Chris's face begins to relax,
As if he's just seen a vision
Crawl out of a tall glass,
Dressed in nothing but mint leaves.
Three or four rounds later,
Everyone is blessedly at peace,
Discussing the fate of the stock market
And its inexplicable turnaround.
All is jolly good, indeed—
Even to the point where Lou and Dan
Mention an upcoming project,
Offering Father Chris a minor role,
If he thinks he can take time off
From the righteous business at hand.
We're ready to order an additional round
When the waiter divulges the sad news;
There's no mint left—

Maybe enough for one last mojito.
Lou and Dan stare each other down,
Their fingers tightly gripping the table.
Father Chris and I ante up
What money we have between us,
Say *adios* and quickly depart—
To the familiar sound of *La Bamba*
And the rumble of drums in the dark.

THE GENTLE MAN

THE GENTLE MAN

In the tender hands
Of the gentle man,
Love grows like a rose
Whose petals open to show
The woman he knows.
And soft is his touch
That strokes her skin—
This slow, kind act
For which she wishes
To grant him forgiveness
The moment he asks it.
She wonders where he learned
The lost art of hesitation,
How kiss and caress differ
In every conceivable way
And why one of his glances
Makes her knees quiver.
Each night she prays
He will never go away,
Leaving her vacant and dry,
Unable to seize the desire
Which waits so patiently
In the tender hands
Of the gentle man.

JERSEY AIR

On the side of Route 4,
Two skunks struck dumb
By a speeding Buick—
Hellbent on reaching home
Before the dinner bell rang.
How is it hope springs
Eternal in the human breast,
But no more in skunk brains
Littering the local highway
This hot summer night.
And of the pair,
One appeared tiny and frail;
The other—perhaps the mother?
May well have known
Their crossing was a bad idea,
But went on nonetheless,
Tossing maternal instinct
Into an abysmal wind—
The smell that lingers
Long past midnight
Through the thick Jersey air.

Bart Edelman

BROKEN HEARTS

He had not yet met
A damaged woman he didn't love.
They came to him
In all sizes and shapes,
And he kept them for months,
Attempting to mend each one,
Before he sent them
Back on the street again.

Here were hungry women
Without names or faces—
Girls who couldn't quite guess
What to make of their lives,
Always watching and praying
For days which never arrived,
Nights leaving nothing more
Than an empty circle of sleep.

So good did he eventually grow
At his collectable craft,
Women stood in line
To plead each separate case.
There was much hand wringing
And the jerking of tears;
Soon he had to add
An extra story to his house.

The neighbors assumed he must be
Some type of petty criminal.
They filed countless complaints,
Alleging he was up to no good,

But it didn't stop him
From filling the floors
With waif-like waitresses
And an occasional obese usherette.

In the end, then,
His home became a hotel
Whose revolving doors opened
To women from around the world.
Here he worshipped a single truth
Behind four granite walls,
Where he lovingly exchanged
One broken heart for another.

BASHEVIS

In a strange tongue
They tell us is mute,
You spoke for those who now
Peddle their gabardine dreams
Six feet beneath the earth.

What Warsaw was then . . .
When Krochmalna Street bustled
With Jew after unsuspecting Jew,
You refused to surrender,
Long after the hateful race
Disfigured each face
And charred hope forever—
A layer of powdered ash.

A swank continent away,
On some unholy day,
You lit the only candle worth saving;
One tiny flame flickered
In a miserable heart.

To say the distant madness
Never touched you in America
Dismisses the dozen dibbuks,
Howling by your back door,
Dying to tear at your soul.

Ah, noble Bashevis—
Spinner of improbable yarns,
Mystical seeker of vision;
Where do you sleep tonight?

Your hairless head heavy,
Your pen poised and ready
To write the family name
Upon every dusty tomb of life.

—*for Isaac Bashevis Singer*

Bart Edelman

THIS CASE FOR YOU

I watch the way you sway
Into the office we share,
Monday, Wednesday and Friday,
Dropping papers, books and exams
Upon the allotted space
I've cleaned for you
Across my empty desk.
You're sighing, yet again,
About the latest tiff,
Telling me, perhaps, it's more—
Some dark funnel cloud
Before the next storm.
You wonder how long
You'll stay with him.

We speak for five minutes
And you dash off to class,
A lecture to deliver on Pynchon.
I hold the novel you gave me—
His first, just to begin—
Smoothing out the torn cover.
I finished reading the book
Over winter vacation,
But don't want to part with it,
Especially the passages you underlined
When once you were a student.
I think of the past three months
And know I've got it bad . . .
This case for you.

I wait a few more moments,
Slipping out of the office

To fetch the morning's mail.
I take the only possible route
Leading me to your classroom.
Through the door's glass window
I find you at the lectern—
Hands softly fanning the air,
As if another germinal idea
Landed safely on your shoulder.
The students follow your every move;
Why wouldn't they, I muse.

Chances are you'll be gone
By next semester's end.
Some doctoral program will surely
Snatch you up in no time
And put you to work for them—
With or without the beau
Who claims he'll follow you
As far as the panhandle.
And what, then, of me?
I'll be left to dwell on days,
When what you wore to work
Kept me dreaming at night.
How your sweet evergreen smell
Clings to the books I love.

U.S.A.

Here, in America,
We never stand on ceremony
But move easily through life,
Taking it all in stride,
One day at a time.
We unfurl the stars and stripes
And elongate the truth—
At all costs—
Because we are free to do so.

Here, in a united America,
We slip into perfect position,
Depending on the issue at hand.
We turn left to center
And center to right—
Sometimes, in the same night,
Striking only when danger
Rears its scaly little head.

Here, in the United Snakes of America,
We slink along on our bellies
And leave each limb to charity;
After all, who needs them?
We detest moral treachery
In the highest office,
Demanding a public execution,
Before we slither off to sleep.

THE GIRL YOU LOVE TO HATE

The girl you love to hate
Strides into the restaurant,
Confident and self-assured.
She's quite tall and lanky
With hair halfway down her back,
And she's wearing no makeup.
The white cotton summer dress
She's selected for the afternoon
Clings to her tan skin and rests
Three inches above her knees.
There's a table already set for her
In the middle of the room,
And you wonder who will join her.

From the corner of your eye
You spy the girl you love to hate,
As her long delicate fingers
Grasp a glass of water,
Raise it to curved lips
You swear must be collagen injected,
Although you know it's not the case.
But this is exactly what
You would tell your best friend
If she were there with you now,
And she would certainly agree.

One by one, heads turn
Towards the girl you love to hate.
Men, women and children
Measure her perfect face,
And stillness fills the room.
A man enters the restaurant

Bart Edelman

In search of the girl who sighs
The moment she sees him
Drop into the chair beside her.

Soon his hand slips between hers,
The clatter of dishes resumes,
And people regain the voices
They traded for beauty's silence.
Amid the afternoon glow
You lower your eyes
When you feel shame's stain
Crawl slowly over you.
Yet the vision of the girl
Refuses to vanish entirely—
And you realize, again,
Just how much you hate her.

PHOTOGRAPH (CIRCA 1960)

You open the freezer one morning
In search of an onion bagel
To suppress last night's hunger,
Finding an old photograph
Hidden among the frozen foods.
You don't question how it got there—
Stranger things have happened;
Rather, you take it in stride
And begin the thawing process.
About an hour or two later
It all comes into focus:
The year is circa 1960,
Your family carefully posed
Around the backyard swimming pool
Which will one day swallow
Your younger brother, Herbert,
Who will lie, motionless,
At the bottom of the deep end,
Before he is discovered by you.
But in the photograph, of course,
There is no sign of this tragedy—
Just you two holding hands,
While your parents sit, lovingly,
On the edge of the diving board.
And that makes you wonder:
Who took this particular picture?
Any clue you hoped to find written
On the back of the snapshot
Has disappeared across the wet surface,
Becoming, more or less, illegible.
This bothers you for a brief moment,
Until you wash a week's worth of dishes
And replace the photograph in the freezer.

Bart Edelman

SO MUCH LIKE MARIE

So much like Marie—
It's how I saw you:
Slender fingers on hips,
Waiting for the crosstown bus
That never arrived to claim you
On the first day of winter,
When I thought, surely,
I must have lost my mind.

And there you stood,
Portrait of a girl
Caught in confusion's midst;
How were you to learn—
How could you possibly tell—
What I chanced upon
Kept the cold lie alive
Another season.

Soon, I followed you down
A strangely familiar block
Where we set up house
On a lot so vacant,
It had no address
And mail failed to find us.

I don't remember the moment
You began to resemble yourself,
Growing into the woman
I refused night after night.
I think I loved you best
When you were anyone—
A prism in my hands—
So much like Marie.

THE CHIEF

The chief hasn't been laid
In well over a year.
He'd like to meet for a drink
To discuss this important matter.
He feels he can't tell
Another soul about his problem;
After all, he is the chief,
And he doesn't really think
He ought to go around
Pleading for a piece of tail.
He stops short of claiming
It should be his given right,
But I know him quite well—
And that's exactly what he thinks.

The chief wants me to assure him
This won't go any further
Than the two of us.
The poor guy's desperate.
Hell, he's had hundreds of women—
Sometimes, three in a single day;
What's happened to him now? he wonders.
Have I noticed anything unusual
About his demeanor or actions,
Deterring women from finding him attractive?
He encourages me to smell his breath,
And I must admit it's rather pleasant.

The chief eagerly asks
If there are any available women
I might set him up with
For an evening this week.

Bart Edelman

Somehow he thinks I have
A pipeline to easy street.
He appears crestfallen
When I tell him I know
No one who would be right
For someone of his position.
Then he lowers his head in shame
And mutters he'd gladly
Wear some type of disguise
Or carry on this little tryst
In another town far away,
Where he's a complete stranger.

In the end, the chief departs—
No better off for having met me.
I agree to make various inquiries,
But he seems a beaten man,
Ordering one too many gin and tonics,
Stumbling out of the bar,
Refusing help to reach home.
And I feel like a failure,
Unable to provide him
The most basic of needs,
So when I dream that night
It's the chief's face I see,
Sadly staring down at me
From some distant star.

IN ALBANY LOVE

In Albany love
Taps me on the shoulder,
And when I whirl around
There you stand, laughing,
Your suitcase packed,
A map in your hand.

In Albany love
Arrives in the middle of spring,
Floating on feathered wings,
Lighter than the breeze
Rolling off the Hudson—
And we catch it just right.

In Albany love
Drops softly from trees,
Blankets the city streets
We walk hour after hour,
In search of a neighborhood
We can both call home.

In Albany love
Allows us to review
The course of history
It took to find us here,
Where we build a little house
On a lot outside Loudonville.

In Albany love
Teaches us how kindness
Is really hope in disguise,
How patience gets a bad rap,
And how nothing in this world
Will ever be the same again.

Bart Edelman

FORGIVENESS

She knows now,
Yet never lets on.
The briefly mentioned name
Rings like any other:
Two syllables lightly pronounced,
An iamb of decency
Fills the friendly kitchen
Where we speak through morning tea.

At another time—
In this same place—
The voices of distant wolves
Were the only company
We kept for years.
Then the irremediable silence,
So stuffed with suffering,
We thought we'd lost it all,
Begging to die
Before the next night fell.

The long trail to forgiveness
Sweeps behind the house we share
And runs along a rocky creek,
Where water gently flows
When rain collects there.
Here, we beat yesterday's clothes
Against the smooth gray stones,
Slowly watching old stains
Drain below the surface.

CHEMISTRY EXPERIMENT

We listened intently to the professor,
Followed each one of her instructions,
Read through the textbook twice,
Wore lab coats and safety goggles,
Mixed the perfect chemical combinations
In the proper amounts and order.
It was all progressing smoothly;
We thought we were a complete success.
And then the flash of light,
The loud, perplexing explosion,
The black rope of smoke,
Rising freely above our singed hair.
Someone in another lab down the hallway
Phoned the local fire department,
Which arrived lickety-split
With the hazardous waste crew,
And they assessed the accident,
Deciding we were out of danger.
It was the talk of the campus
For many weeks afterwards.
We, however, became so disillusioned,
We immediately dropped the course,
Gradually retreating from each other.
The very idea we could have done
More damage than we actually did—
Blown up ourselves and the building
From the base of its foundation—
Shook us, like nothing had before.
And even now, years later,
When anyone still asks about you,
I get this sick feeling in my stomach,
Wondering what really happened
To all that elementary matter.

Bart Edelman

YOUR FATHER'S GHOST

I tried—really I did—
To crawl into your life
And make sense of madness
I was unable to comprehend.
Through the small Southwestern towns,
Across the great state of Texas,
I chased your father's ghost,
Never very far behind.
Traveling east on Interstate 10—
Driving home to Lafayette—
I asked him why . . . why . . . why . . .
But he refused to answer;
His lips, twisted and fixed
On the asphalt ahead of him,
Counting each mile as if it were
The last step towards execution.
I can well imagine,
His soberest day came
When they took you away
And gave you another man's name.
He must have been dead, then,
Before the ink dried on the document,
Yet he would have five long years
To test the depth of his sorrow
At the bottom of a bottle.
As for you, sweet girl,
The past is often unkind
To an innocent child
Along for the ride.

POETRY (IN MOTION)

A student sitting in my office
Is privy to a conversation
I have with my publisher.
Through a strange quirk of fate
Harley-Davidson offers, possibly,
To ante up bucks for my new book—
Something about improving their image
By taking the literary high road.
How cool, the young woman coos.
That's so unbelievably awesome.
Will they put a picture of you
On the back of a bike?
I tell her quite frankly
This remains to be seen.
We have no sign of money yet—
Only the word of an underling
Who wants a manuscript
Sent to his office,
Somewhere in Illinois,
By this time next week.
Where the hell is Illinois?
The inquisitive student wonders.
I think a geography course
With the dynamic Professor Leaver
May do her more good
Than the current poetry class
She visits rather infrequently.
Soon she is on her way,
All filled up by alliteration
And a dash of caesura—for good measure.
I'm left with a curious image of me,
Straddling some red metallic hog,

Bart Edelman

Dressed from head to toe in black leather,
A rather disconcerting thought.
But, then again,
Things could fare far worse;
I could be perfectly posed
Behind the wheel of my father's Oldsmobile,
Driving the sleek General Motors' dream,
Deep into the new millennium.

DANGEROUS CURVE

Just up ahead,
Slightly around the bend,
The road dips down
A country two-lane blacktop,
And there she stands
Under the summer moon,
Staring at the sky,
Swimming with silver stars.
She sways to the sound
The wind makes as it slaps
The corn back and forth
Across the open field—
Body in motion,
Heart at rest.
She knows she must leave
This place where nothing grows
Inside her tiny heart
But a dry stalk of grief
She snaps day after day,
Praying for another soul
To share her desolation—
If only for the moment it takes
Until the approaching car
Flashes its high beams
And hurtles to meet her.

Bart Edelman

LOSING OLIVIA

You could have told me
I wasn't the one for you;
It would have saved time
And a lesson in grief
I learned far too late.

You could have told me
We really had no chance,
For I was clueless—
Odd as it may seem—
I'm a bit foolish that way.

You could have told me
Just how silly I appeared,
Trailing after you each night,
A chrysanthemum in my hand—
This stupid song on my lips.

You could have told me
What happens to poor souls
Who leave their hearts out
Too long in the rain,
And fail to find them again.

You could have told me
Love is a fickle thing
I had no right believing in;
That's what I wish you said:
But, Liv, you never did.

70

It was the one season
He'd dreamed of his entire life,
An eternal summer when the ball
Floated towards home plate
As big as a grapefruit.
He squarely planted his feet,
Pointed his bat skyward,
And waited for the chance
To launch another long drive
Beyond the outfield fence,
Where fans gathered to catch
History in their hands.

The pitcher's deliberate pace
Did nothing to unnerve him;
He knew the routine by now—
How not even a patron saint
Wanted his name left to rot
In the sacred record book
For future generations to read,
As the poor, unfortunate soul
Who made this moment possible.

He stepped out of the box,
Knocked some dirt from his spikes,
Adjusted the cap bearing
The name of the city he loved,
And heard his father's voice,
Coaxing him to relax,
Take a deep breath:
Remember, this is just a game
Children play for fun.

Bart Edelman

Then came the wind-up . . .
One arm twisting overhead,
The release which sent the sphere
Rapidly spinning for home.
Later, he swore he saw
Each minute revolution
Before the crack of bat to ball—
The great row of faces,
Straining to follow the flight
One man made in early October,
On a hazy Sunday afternoon,
When he dared to chase
Time and alter space.

—*for Mark McGwire*

REQUEST

Just one request—
It's all I ask—
A small act of kindness
I wish to remember you by,
When winter slips into spring
And we stand no more,
Huddled against the stiff wind
This time of year brings.

Please don't let them know
How it was we came
To love each other;
Why yours were the arms
I chose to wrap around me—
A shawl of forgiveness
I wore to brace the cold.

And don't tell woeful tales,
Trapping the truth in lies,
Where body and soul collide
Under the sad guise of reason.
Step gently away from temptation—
The profane urge to shed
What little remains of our skin.

THE ALPHABET OF LOVE

THE ALPHABET OF LOVE

A adores B,
But B is enamored with C.
C suffers terribly
From a protracted divorce with D
And won't get involved with anyone now;
However, C thinks E is fun
To help break the weekend monotony.
E seems mixed-up
And fell for F
Last month at a dance ranch,
Yet wonders why C hangs around.
Maybe G, a friend's sister,
Would be the best bet of all,
Since the family is wealthy,
But E really has the hots for H,
Who runs around the track
Each week with I and J.
They both seem happily married to K and L,
Although H knows the score:
I carries on at the office with M,
And J spends each spare moment with N,
When not making plans with O.
H thinks of lying low for a while,
Knowing full well P
Would take him back in a second.
(P wouldn't want him back again
For all the tea in China,
Yet how could H know this?)
P is, in fact, being slandered by Q,
Who's upset by P's comportment
And lack of moral candor.
Q has decided to remain chaste—
The only way to go these days—

And thinks R, a former mate,
Might do well to heed the same words.
R entertained S and T
On consecutive evenings,
Feeling no shame whatsoever.
R advises Q that it's fine to play alone;
Everyone ought to have a choice.
Just the same though,
Perhaps, he might be willing
To speak to someone like U,
Who has a thriving practice
Over on the Westside of town.
After all, didn't they both date V,
When they were in high school?
And speaking of V,
Wasn't that she on television last night
Throwing herself all over W,
Who walked out on X and their four children—
Despite the fact that they apparently
Had patched things up
Over W's affair with Y
(According to People magazine).
No, V is truly a blockhead
And was never happier than the time
She and Z worked for the circus
(As jugglers and clowns),
When they lived in Manhattan.
If only Z hadn't taken that role
In the movie which filmed
On Bora Bora, starring A,
Everything would have been so simple—
But that was, alas,
Long before A came to adore B.

Bart Edelman

BLACK PEARLS

From the bottom of the sea
Twelve black pearls
Sang to me,
Each voice an octave
Higher than the next.
A dozen depths I dove—
Devoid of breath—
Closer to the precious stones
Upon the ocean floor.
Was I the first to see
This midnight cluster
Dance across the waves
And steal between the stars?
Carefully, I touched each gem,
Feeling the smooth, round skin
Roll slowly into my palm.
Dare I even ask
What divine creature
Opened its shell
To such perfect mystery?
And yet I knew
I did not possess
Either jewel, or key,
From which I could unlock
Ancient symmetry.
Under the shadow of glass
I floated a moment more,
Before I swam to the surface,
Empty-handed—
My fingers glowing in the dark.

From the bottom of the sea
Twelve black pearls
Sang to me.

BONES OF SILENCE

Once, each season,
When barking voices give way
To bones of silence,
I listen closely
For proof I'm still alive.
I dig a six foot hole
In the cold, dark earth
And bury myself
Among the tightly packed pockets,
Forming a perpetual line
Across my backyard.

After an hour, perhaps two,
The first sound I hear underground
Is nothing more than the truth,
Burrowing slowly towards me—
A timeless tunnel
Tracing the empty space
Between yesterday and today;
This constant struggle which pits
The forces of then
Against the wisdom of now.

Before long I sense
Cautious movement around me;
Small creatures take care
Not to disturb my resting place,
As if they know the secret peace
Lodging beneath the soil.
Soon, I am enveloped in sleep—

Bart Edelman

Deep enough to forget my name.
I awake the next morning
To the strain of a wailing howl,
And rise early—
Only to gnaw again.

THE BOOK OF LIFE

He had cultivated
Love in a windowbox,
So high above the city
He never saw the street.
Daily, his patient fingers
Nurtured the soil,
And watched seed
Slowly turn to stalk,
Stem become flower.
Here was goodness
He could hold
In the palm of his hand,
Bright sunlight which danced
Down a deserted hallway,
And crept across
The drab little room,
Where, page by page,
He pressed each precious petal
Into the book of life.

THE CROW'S NEST

The crow came soon
To rest among feathers—
Cool to the claw,
Warm on the wing.

The crow did not know
How long it had been,
Since this downy bed
Tucked another bird
In the soft grasp of spring.

For all the crow cared,
It may well have taken
Nine beaks to build the nest,
But it was of no consequence.

When a lonely crow
Measures the black stars
Against a glass sky,
Nothing can safely pass
Between night and sleep.

THE DANCER

Watch her begin to spin,
Turning circles in the air,
Floating like a feather
On the back of the wind.
Come, take a moment
To sit and observe:
The tilt of her head,
The swirl of her lips,
The sweep of her hands,
The curl of her hips.
See how rivers flow
Beneath her knees;
Lush gardens grow
Up through her toes.
Feel the beat of the street
As both feet kiss the floor,
Her city, never at rest.
And always there is undulation—
This perpetual motion—
Marriage of beauty to form,
Graceful strength newly born.

Bart Edelman

DAY OF THE LOCUS

Amid the discarded shards of hope,
Twinkling glass shattered the roadway,
Cradling Route 111 and Route 80
In the palm of a giant, unforgiving hand,
Closing between Calexico and El Centro.
There wasn't even a moment
For them to say goodbye.

Eileen's watch stopped at 2:55
On December 22, 1940.
She lay twisted in a ditch,
While Nat toiled with his last breath,
Gasping on the asphalt.

For both of them
Time ceased to exist.
Gone were the books, the hunting trips,
And the children who would never be.
The wedding dishes, still packed,
Sat at home in boxes,
As if they somehow knew
Destiny had no business eating breakfast.

They had waited a lifetime for each other,
And now West had failed
To yield the right of way,
Ignoring the only glaring sign
On that Sunday afternoon,
Trading his belief in the party dress
For the politics of the open road,
Dangling behind the lethal wheel.

And when it came to pass,
It certainly wasn't the crash
Of the 30s that killed them,
But a Pontiac sedan
Driven by a fruit tramp
Whose hand West would have gladly shaken
On any given night.

For what ultimate purpose
Was the locus of fate formed,
If not to crack the clock,
Bleeding drop by drop,
Out along the lonely boulevard.

Had the gods bothered to look down
That cool winter day,
They might have seen
A million teeming dreams
Rising up to meet them.

—for Nathanael West

Bart Edelman

THE DOGS OF AMADEUS

The dogs of Amadeus
Bark night and day,
Now that the master's away.
You can hear them yelp
Clear across the valley
And over the next hill.
The scent from his skin remains,
But this is not enough
To make the creatures sane.
Only when we play his music,
Do they lay their heads
Upon the cold ground,
Crying themselves to sleep.
Why he need keep
So many hounds around
Confounds each one of us.
Perhaps, it is better
Not to know such things.
When spring finally arrives,
And he returns again,
All shall be well—
The dogs will wag their tails,
Growing silent at his feet,
While we complete
What must be done,
If he is to compose the work
The world will one day hear.

EAST MEETS WEST

Someone's been writing verse
Across the stark white walls
Outside the City Hall of Kiev.
Such words tell stories,
Hellbent on hope:
This is what is—
That was what was.
People, once shy and silent,
Slip pens in their pockets,
Take the metro uptown
To add a stanza or two,
Before the querulous old guard
Comes snooping around the corner.
Everyone's a poet these days,
Sneers the deputy minister;
But even he scrawls his message
On the clean flat surface,
When he's alone at night—
After the sun sets—
And east meets west.

FOOTSTEPS

If I listen closely enough,
I can hear your father's footsteps
Gaining on you each day;
Sometimes, it's how you say your name
Or the way you tilt your head—
Side to side—
The subtle act of denial,
Turning your smile upside down.

And when life runs too smoothly,
You retreat to the kitchen's corner
As if you're waiting
For the next shoe to drop,
The open hand to fall,
Slapping you across the room.

Once, I admit,
I had the thought,
Perhaps, things would work
Better between us
If I just played the part,
Kept the lie alive,
Twisting my tongue
Into a series of knots,
Swallowing these dirty little secrets—
One by one.

And he's coming next week
On the train from Florida,
Bringing with him
His eighth wife,
His mountain of debt,

His outstanding warrants,
And, of course, his bottle,
From which he'll pour you
A tall glass of shame.
And you will do nothing
To send him away,
For fear you'll lose
The tight-fisted glove,
Gripping his terrible love.

THE GREAT DARK

Agleam, aglitter, aglow—
Even the faintest star
Always knows how far
To cast its light
Around the unsuspecting moon.
What little hope remains:
We tuck inside a pocket,
Seal within an envelope,
Lock behind a door.
And, still, there's no guarantee,
Whatever it is we see
Illuminates the great dark.
Could the firefly speak,
She would reveal
The story of her life,
Where day becomes night
With just the sudden flick
Of an internal switch.
If only it were that simple
For the rest of us,
Caught somewhere in midair,
Flying through the gloom—
Our fluorescent search begun,
Love's labor never done.

THE LATE NATALIE WOOD

I saw the late Natalie Wood
At Christmas Eve Mass last night
In the Church of the Good Shepherd,
Smack dab on Bedford Drive,
In the heart of Beverly Hills;
How curious to see her alive again!
There were flowers in her hand,
And she was wearing
A splendid black Chanel jacket,
And a lavender jacquard skirt.
At her side sat a man
No more than twenty years old,
Transfixed beyond measure,
Staring unabashedly at her,
Running his eyes through her hair—
From the opening rite
To the closing prayer.
Even normally cool Father O'Ryan
Seemed a bit taken aback
With the vision in the front pew,
But he couldn't place
Where he'd seen that face before . . .
Still, his intrigue remained
Until the final carol was sung,
The chant of peace exchanged.
When Natalie Wood rose to leave,
We stood there silently,
Watching her stroll up the aisle,
Smiling at each one of us,
As if we had just been blessed
By the mere sight of her,

Bart Edelman

Passing through our lives
On this most holy night,
Where she suddenly appeared
To worship the birth of Christ.

LITTLE GHOSTS

This overwhelming sense of dread,
Damp tendrils wrapped tightly
Around children's heads;
Two doors slam shut,
And she bolts up in bed.

It is midnight in Prague—
Bleary eyed, she leaves her room.
The front desk manager
Takes one glance at her,
Knowing where she's been.
He offers her tea
And leaves an extra glass out.
It is for the little ghosts, he says,
The children who slept here
Days before they were sent to Terezin,
Later to find their fate at Auschwitz.

You see, he explains,
This was once a way station.
The young ones were kept at this place
Prior to their deportation.
They were, indeed, orphans,
The poor unfortunates who died twice—
First, when their parents were led away
Or shot in the street,
And, again, when the Gestapo
Trapped them behind these walls.
He states this rather methodically,
Without surprise to find her
Wandering sleepless at this hour.
It is the malady of many

Bart Edelman

Who unknowingly board here.
The little ghosts reveal themselves
Only to the ears and eyes of strangers.

The next morning
She approaches the desk
To check out early.
The manager has her bill calculated
Before a word is spoken.
She detects his wry smile
And hears a small voice call
As she steps into the past—
A familiar train at her back,
Belching smoke down the tracks.

THE LOCKET

Oh, to be encased
Inside a heart-shaped locket,
Gently resting below the neck
Of the woman I love,
So she is free to see me
Whenever it pleases her.
There I would wait patiently
By light of day,
Or dark of night,
Just for a single kiss
And the warm breath
Escaping her lips.
Within a closed hand
She would clasp me tightly,
Then slowly open the catch,
Revealing the only man
She can trust enough
To share her secret life—
Tender dreams of hope
She takes to bed each night.
With a delicate finger
And a wistful sigh,
I watch her carefully trace
The contour of my tiny face,
Before she shuts the case,
Tucking me safely away—
For another day.

Bart Edelman

MARK TWAIN'S CIGAR

Mark Twain's cigar
Glows in winter's gloom;
By a dim light,
Ringing the dark side of the moon,
He carefully writes,
How poor am I
Who was once so rich!
And closes the notebook
He will later call his autobiography.
Before he climbs into bed,
He pours a jigger of brandy—
Prescribed by the doctor for his heart—
And drops slowly off to sleep.

In the recurring shadow,
Revealing a remarkable dream,
Five coffins await him
When he descends the stairs
And enters the kitchen for breakfast.
One by one, he reads the placards
Which sit beside the caskets,
But they make absolutely no sense.
Bending over the open boxes,
He finds each is empty,
Except for some unrecognizable photographs
Meaning nothing to him—
Strange faces in silent rivers.

Returning home, later that day,
He is alarmed to discover
The coffins are now cradles,

And the servants gently rock them,
Singing hymns as if they were in church.
Angrily, he demands the small beds be removed—
Yet then thinks better of it,
Realizing the wood can be put to good use;
He suggests it be immediately cut
And stacked in the carriage house.
The servants stare at him in horror,
But he can not understand their amazement
At such a simple and reasonable request.

Mark Twain awakes the next morning,
Dressed in yesterday's clothes,
Closely watching the angels
Carved in the magnificent headboard
He brought back from Europe.
Scattered ashes of regret
Lie across the oversized bed,
His mouth parched and thirsty
From the faint taste of tobacco leaves.
A half-smoked cigar
Rests in his right hand,
And he seems quite surprised
To find himself alive.

Bart Edelman

NAMES

Say your name twice,
Repeating each syllable
Softly and slowly, at first,
As if the world would be
A lonely space without it.
Ask yourself why
You were given this name
And trace it
On the back of a leaf,
Or down the edge of a stem,
Touching every letter
With the tip of your tongue.
Now, wonder aloud
What you would lose
And who you would be
If this familiar name
No longer belonged to you
And was bartered away
On the price of a song.
For when life seems too busy
With people and places and things,
Making you question
Why you are here,
Then write your name
In the warm rain
The night left behind,
And always know
It will be waiting
To follow you home.

THE NEW TRAIN

The new train travels
Swiftly over tarnished tracks,
Budapest no longer some distant dream
Or dot on a map.
Time slides back to reveal
The rolling hills of spring,
Caught midway between seasons—
Too sleepy for change.

Just outside of Brno,
Daisies grow wild in the sun
And cover mile after mile—
A carpet of golden hope—
As far as the eye can see.

At Breclav, a young transit policeman
Asks for proof of citizenship,
Decidedly eager to show
His proficient use of English;
He checks our passports,
Laughing at the photographs.

Time wanes and turns to haze.
In the glass corridor
Where forgotten dreams remain,
We reason why we journey here,
Crossing each silent bridge—
A trestle closer to tomorrow.

Approaching curious Bratislava,
The new voice of Slovakia
Whispers a clever secret

Out among the green fields
And tiny vineyards stretching
Along the gentle slopes,
Winding through the countryside.

With Budapest on the horizon
And the Danube's blue water
Curled like a child beside us,
We ride into the heart of Hungary,
Tracing our way home—
One rail at a time.

THE POLICEMAN'S WIFE

The policeman's wife
Shadows me across the room,
Searching for clues
In every line I read.
She watches me—
Week after week—
Counting down each day
Until the semester snaps shut,
A hungry set of jaws.

The policeman's wife
Thinks I ought to know
What she was before,
And what she is today.
The power of the word
Has turned her loose
To walk the naked streets,
Her only crime her skin—
A rash of wasted time.

The policeman's wife
Quivers ever so slightly
When she talks to me.
She sits in my office,
Her hand brushing my knee,
And I anticipate our future:
How many laws would we break?
How many states would we flee?
How soon would he find me?

The policeman's wife
Plans a secret rendezvous

Bart Edelman

Out along Highway 321,
One week after the term ends.
Are you game? she asks by phone.
The offer sounds tantalizing,
But I weigh eternity behind bars
And cop a pitiful plea,
Before I blot her out of my life.

WHITE BIRD

And even when you know
There's no chance of hope,
You still can't let go.
You wash your hands,
Over and over,
Yet the heart
Never takes well
To a cake of soap
And a basin of water.
Here, a strange new pain,
Though localized at first,
Spreads slowly from limb to limb,
Until you feel, surely,
This body is not your own.
And how could it be,
When there is nothing
More to touch
But a hard shell
Covering a frozen field.
Somewhere above the tundra,
Foolish voices can be heard
Whispering of seasons to come;
Down the distant hallway,
In a room designed for living,
A man speaks a language
A woman actually understands—
Simple words, empty space.
And love is a white bird
With a shattered beak,
A broken wing.

Bart Edelman

UNDER DAMARIS' DRESS

UNDER DAMARIS' DRESS

Under Damaris' dress
I crept that cold night
To watch the crackling firelight
Burn between her legs.
White winter snow dropped flakes
Against the windowpane,
And inside I remained
To cross the orange lake.
My trembling hands she covered,
My wild eyes she closed,
With only words that she would know
She taught me how to love her.
We lay so near, the fear so far,
I felt my life unfold,
On silken sheets, in tents of gold,
I caught a falling star.
Her gentle touch, her soft caress,
From these I must confess,
I learned the art of tenderness
Under Damaris' dress.

EARTHQUAKE / LOS ANGELES

We wake at 4:31 A.M.
To the shake of crashing objects,
Here a plate,
There a frame,
Everywhere the sound of breaking glass.
The earth rocks and rolls,
And we hang on
To what stands still.
All day,
Tremor after tremor,
Jolt by jolt,
The aftershocks knock us
Back and forth.
We take cover and pray
There are more than enough
Doorways to go around.
Helicopters hover above the houses,
Down the blocks,
Rattling more floors,
Wobbling walls;
Will anything ever be the same?
We listen to Kate Hutton
And her magic seismograph,
Trying to find sense in it all
(At least for the children's sake).
Through the restless night,
We wonder what makes us quake
Before the dawn explodes again—
Yet the age old question . . .
Who shall survive?

—*1/17/94*

Bart Edelman

DAYTONA JONES

My name is Daytona Jones,
And I'm not a car, a city or a speedway . . .
The new girl in town
Plopped down in her chair
And sobbed,
Tear after tear
Dropped on her wooden desk;
We hadn't said a word—
Never got the chance.

Daytona Jones:
Slight, very slight,
Blue ribbons
Tied in crinkly hair,
Pink dress,
White shoes,
Brown skin—
The color of coffee beans
Roasted over an open fire.

Daytona Jones:
Always alone,
One month,
Two at the most;
She was gone
Before she came—
A hollow reed on the wind—
Leaving her name,
And the only words she ever spoke.

THE CABLE

We bait the hook,
Hanging from our rod,
Cast the line out to water,
Sit still in our little boat,
Wait for a bite.
There is the passage of time,
When the mind meanders
Down below the surface,
Back up for air,
Always aware of any nibble.
A slight tug is cause for elation.
The taut cord pulsates.
We hold the cable tight . . .
Listen to it sing.

Bart Edelman

NOW THAT SHE HAS GONE

Now that she has gone
You look at the bed
Where you both slept
And know it no longer
Belongs to you.
You think of sending it to her,
But the freight would be exorbitant.
This makes you chuckle,
Until you begin to cry.
Death does not come easy
To grown men caught falling
Through the trapdoor of love.

When you find a note she wrote,
A photograph,
An errant sock,
A lock of hair,
You carry it outside
To discard in the trash,
Burying it
Among the dust and lint
She left behind . . .
If you can't have her,
Nobody will.

She has touched
Every plate, pot and pan
In your vacant museum.
You are not hungry
But crack an egg to scramble,
Toast a slice of bread—

Your diet for a month now.
You taste nothing,
Only your parched throat,
And dare not meddle with the ritual.

You tell the friends who call,
You are chronically unemployed;
There isn't any work
For a man with your skills—
Besides, no one hires
A walking cross these days.

Should it lift one morning,
You will confess to her
How much she taught you;
Perhaps, there may be a meeting
In some public place,
A formal apology or two.
And later that night
You will begin to learn
The tenure of regret.

Bart Edelman

ENGLISH 101

They appear—
Always—
That first day,
Astray;
Some wait to fall,
Others to rise:

Here rests the tired boy,
The hour long,
He drops his brain
Upon the desk
And thinks he'd be better off dead,
Five worlds away
From Frost and Twain . . .
(He'll have no part of 101).

A fair-haired girl in knots
Twists her braids so tight
They make her ache;
She takes good notes,
Does what she's told,
If asked a quote
She knows it cold . . .
(But could a smile unclench those lips?)

Then the hand,
One resolute voice
Speaks through the bell
And the great stampede—
Engaged in speculation
We turn wheat to notion,
Sifting through each tiny grain . . .
(The composition now complete).

COURTSHIP

I wanted to walk you to school,
But you said, suddenly, you felt ill.

I wanted to hold your hand,
But you said you had a bum leg.

I wanted to kiss you,
But you said that was unthinkable.

I wanted to comb your hair,
But you said you hid the brush.

I wanted to paint your fingernails,
But you said you'd bit them down to nothing.

I wanted to search for answers,
But you said I hadn't a clue.

I wanted to wash your feet,
But you said I was unclean.

I wanted to make love to you last night,
But you said you were a morning person.

I wanted to make love to you this morning,
But you said it was too early in the day.

I wanted to take you away on a vacation,
But you said you'd rather stay at home.

I wanted to set the record straight,
But you said you liked it crooked.

Bart Edelman

I wanted to have a serious conversation,
But you said I was being silly.

Then I asked you to marry me,
And you said, yes, of course.

BLACK CADILLAC

The elongated fins,
A flying fish on wheels—
Grandpa's shiny new Cadillac
Floated down the block at twilight,
Beached itself on the concrete sand.
Three toots of the horn
Brought us screaming from the house;
We swept around the immaculate sedan
And gazed in astonishment . . .
He'd really done it this time.

Grandpa stood in his pinstriped suit
With his back to us,
Whistling *Take Me Out To The Ballgame,*
Smoking a Tareyton.
He jingled a pocketful of change,
Stroked a long string of keys
And turned towards us, grinning.
So what do you think?
Anyone up for a ride?
It's only the shank of the evening.
I think we need to go nightlifin'.
Get inside and put your pajamas on.
We'll be out 'til the wee hours.

Past the frown on Mother's face we dashed,
Ready for adventure.
From our bedroom we heard
The exchange of raised voices,
Cross words,
A painful drawn out sigh,

Bart Edelman

Then nothing but silence,
And an engine ignited.

By the time we reached the street,
He was gone;
We could barely make out
The slippery tail
Flipping in the wind,
Swimming far out to sea
As if it had never been there.
Mother told us calmly
He had other stops to make,
But we knew the reason he didn't stay—
Why she always chased him away.

Months later,
When Grandpa came calling for us,
Willing to explain,
He was driving an old brown Chevrolet.

DEAD CHICKEN

We're arguing again,
And I say
A dead chicken is better
Than no chicken at all,
And you scream
What happened to the egg?
I think you don't get it.
We're crossing two different roads—
No sense going further.
Then the back door
Scratches and moans.
I'd just as soon
Dropkick the cat to Cleveland,
But he's one of your foundlings,
So I let him in,
Bleeding, his left ear half torn,
Some skirmish he's survived.
You rush to comfort him,
Cleaning the wound,
Bundling him up
For another drive to the animal hospital.
You leave without a word.
I hear the car tires
Crunch the snow
And the broken muffler
Coughing down the street.
(It really ought to be fixed
One of these days.)
I climb the stairs,
Marching off to bed,
Awaiting winter's end:
Without chicken, egg, or wife.

Bart Edelman

ECLIPSE

Chained to our chairs,
Burning cigarette after cigarette,
Trails of smoke
Twisted under the wanton sky.
We spoke of Halley's comet,
The lunar eclipse,
Satellites spinning above,
A universe in constant motion . . .
But nothing changed much
When it came to us.
Through tethered lines
We tried to walk
And talk it out again,
As if speech alone could steer us
Nearer to our destination,
Constellation by constellation.
Yet we were always
One star away from each other,
Lost somewhere in the gloom,
Floating through filtered space,
Searching for the miracle—
A silver ship to board
And fly safely home.
In the end all was lost:
Charts, craft, crew,
Disappeared into the charcoal night,
Where we sat mutely,
Plucking the moon from our teeth.

CANCER

Before the mirror
She stands sobbing
In her hospital gown.
I walk towards the bathroom,
Find her tracing the incision's trail
Stretching under her breast,
Across the chest
And up her back.
She motions me closer:
Come see what they've done.
My God . . .
Can this really be me?
I look down at the black lariat
Wound around her body—
A barbed wire fence
To corral the cancer.
I do not shy
But wait until she is ready
For me to dress her
In this disease modesty forbids.
I help her into bed,
Tuck the blanket under her chin,
Ask what else I can do.
My mother rears her head,
Like a startled horse,
Staring above me,
Counting the cracks in the ceiling.

Bart Edelman

IF IT IS

If it is
As you say—
That I will be
The first to find you
And hear the words
You've always wished to speak,
Then I will wait
Week by week,
Silent in my forest,
Deaf to the falling trees,
Blind to the eye of death.

If it is
As you say—
That I will be
The last to touch you
And feel my fingers on your skin,
Then I will wait
Through this long winter,
Face turned to the wind,
Hands pressed in my pockets,
Feet steady on the ground.

If it is
As you say—
That I will be
The only one to love you
And grow old
Holding your dear, sweet face,
Then I will wait
Year after year,
Knowing how faith comes home,
Building this fire in my heart,
Learning to whisper your name.

THE OPEN WINDOW

I keep my window open
To hear the birds
Warbling in the trees,
So many sounds—
Who could count them all?
At daybreak it's clear . . .
I will leave my work behind;
Someone else can do the chore.
I part the shutters,
Let the light
Guide me to my chair.

How curious,
Spending dawn to dusk
Seated here alone
In my silent spring,
Listening to songs
Leap from limb to limb.
Patiently, I await
The chance to join in.

By candleglow,
The nightly migration begins.
The last shadow of flight
Drops from its perch
And wings westward.
I cook a pot of stew,
Pour a cup of tea,
Lean towards awakening.

Bart Edelman

HEARTLAND

In this part of the country,
Sector 25-H,
The Great Midwest,
Nothing passes for love . . .
All dispossessed hearts
Are stored in 777 silos
Stretching skyward.

**

They say they're saving hearts
For a righteous time,
And they've tattooed numbers
In every chamber,
On each atrium,
Just for our own good,
And we'll know
Who's who and what's what
When the moment comes.

**

The epidemic spreads east and west,
Far from the heartland.
No one's safe nowadays—
There's little chance of cure,
Even less of care.
And the dreadful tales they tell:
If you're standing at the right place,
At the wrong time,
They'll rip your heart out;
It's a science I tell you.

**

No one dares
Speak the truth anymore.
Few remain in touch
And those of us with a pulse
Keep this throbbing thing
We call life—to ourselves.
Believe me,
It's dangerous business
Walking through town
With one of these tickers in you.

**

In this part of the country,
Sector 25-H,
The Great Midwest,
Nothing passes for love . . .
Soon there will come
A knock on the door,
A blade at the breast,
And it will be my heart
They'll want to claim and stack.
Until then,
I carry this block of ice
Strapped to my chest,
Lest I explode.

Bart Edelman

WHEN YOU'RE AWAY

When you're away,
I'm out of sync,
Just a bit off,
So friends say,
Who offer company
And plead to cook for me,
Anything I might need—
But I won't have it.

I tinker around the house
To shrink each day
And pace the yard,
Stepping on jagged stones
That grow larger
When I'm alone—
I no longer walk barefoot.

The peacock misses you
And will not fan his feathers,
Shrieking so loudly
It is foolish of me
To think I could write a line—
Even the dogs
Don't come near me
Except to be fed.

Late at night,
In our wide bed,
I drift from side to side,
Never quite finding sleep,
Stirred by unfamiliar sounds

I cannot place,
And stumbling under stars
I trace them one by one,
The moon my only canopy—
When you're away.

BROTHER

Brother—
This withered picture of you
I hold in my hand
Is what I have,
All that remains,
One snapshot of you in overalls,
A smile I carry with me
Year after year.

Brother—
They've posed you
Sitting in the windowcase,
A balancing act of sorts,
One hand clasping a top,
The other waving.
I'd long forgotten
Fingers could be so tiny.

Brother—
I wonder what the day was like.
Were there clouds in the sky?
Sounds of sirens from the distance?
Could I tell, even then,
I would lose you so soon?

Brother—
There was no time
For me to know you
But through hushed words,
A haunted stare into space
Where I tried to find you,

Again and again,
As if you could crawl to me
Out of the heaven that swallowed you.

Brother—
Thank you for the breath of life,
Passing so early from us,
Unaware hope was always alive,
Surviving among us, still.

Bart Edelman

200 KISSES

200 kisses—
We numbered every one,
No two the same.
I am thinking of them now
And the sweet fragrance
Lingering from your skin,
The summer dress
Clinging to the antique chair,
And your bonnet at rest
By the foot of the bed.
You have gone for the night,
But this desire remains.

At work,
Beneath the cool antiseptic glow
And the polished floors,
I can hear them
Asking about the day
And where you go.
What shall you say?
How many clever ways are there
To disguise our love?

I will not stir
From where we lay—
My hands vacant,
My lips dry.
I see your face,
The curl of your smile,
And know why
I still believe in angels,

Beating back the wind—
Their delicate wings on fire.

I listen closely
For the sound of key in lock,
This world spinning like a gyre,
And live to count
Each moment with you,
Kiss by kiss by kiss.

Bart Edelman

CROSSING THE HACKENSACK

CROSSING THE HACKENSACK

Crossing the Hackensack
In dugout canoes,
We lay low,
Crouched and confined,
Placid water rippling beneath us,
Silent paddles sweeping dreams
Below the shadowy surface.
Long we drifted,
Down river in darkness,
Secrets safely stowed,
Courage our sole cargo.
Closer and closer the banks became.
Bravely we scanned treetops
Among the Teaneck timberland,
Searching for a sign of life,
Hoping to heed a sound,
Familiar, faint,
Awaiting Indians along the shore.
Only the lone cricket's chirp
Met us floating toward land,
Our tired hands laden with gifts,
Clutching plastic trinkets and treasures—
Traders of a new age.

Dawn pressed the water's edge,
Stirring us from restless slumber,
Humbling the sojourn we sought.
Emptiness graced the ground.
In either direction space stretched
From one end of the earth to the other—
A canvas of desolation.
If not for youthful wisdom

We might have remained there forever,
Huddled together,
Splinter to splinter,
Fighting off frost and morning dew,
Stuck with the vision of Geronimo.
But slowly we retreated—
Homeward bound,
Pushing our paddles out from sludgy banks,
Embarking on safe passage.

Crossing the Hackensack
In dugout canoes,
We sat erect,
Charting the course before us,
Waiting still . . . waiting still . . .

LOVING YOU

I do not know from where such passion flows.
Always by surprise,
Never the same way twice,
I'm taken—
To love you is still a mystery.
I think of years together,
Building lives like barns,
Our common ways—
Acorns once were we.
But others possess far longer spans;
Time's never a measure of the heart,
Devotion not calibrated,
A worn tire.
No, there's little in all this
To explain the whispered romance,
A longing that renews us.
Beyond youth this yearning grows,
For we are slow in tender ways,
And make love eternally nowadays.

THE HARPER RETURNS

To pattern a life—
A deed worth dying for.
In the mother tongue of a father's heart,
A word forever spoken,
A blessing more noble
Than the only son at dawn,
Dangling on a cross.

With wood and wire and glue—
This is how it is done:
Piece by piece,
A temple on a strand of porous sand,
A church in the midnight sun.
Strike your hammer on every golden nail,
Singing hymn after hymn.

And it is never complete:
Reeds bend in a wind,
Dancers dispense with the dance,
A steady strain drops beyond the vale,
One lone voice echoes . . . an emerald glen.
Still, the architect stretches silver strings
Across the shores where once Cuchulain walked.

—for Dennis Doyle

Bart Edelman

I HURLED YOU DOWN THE RAVINE TODAY

1

I hurled you down the ravine today,
Rain pelting me,
Accomplice to my plan—
The only choice I had
To spare myself another night.

2

I watched you roll,
Blonde braids twirling in the wind,
Black suede skirt on pale skin,
Your bittersweet pride—
My twisted smile.

3

I stood, anchored to the spot,
Awaiting the flat, fatal thud of body to rock,
But a couple passed nearby,
And I fled, slowly,
To avoid attention.

4

The ride home would have pleased you;
I whispered your name endlessly.
All our haunts beckoning,
I treated myself to something sweet:
A cherry tart to remember you.

5

I imagine you're quite dead now,
As I sit in my cozy room,
Open book on my lap;
Hours have passed,
And I feel no guilt.

6

What a beauty you were this morning,
Shameless, before the mirror.
Pity we had to say goodbye
And went our separate ways.
Sleep soundly, my dear—I will.

Bart Edelman

976-STAR

I'm 5'6", long dark hair, 130 lbs.
I've got a great set of boobs
You'd die for,
And I'm hot already,
Star pants into the phone,
While she paints her toenails
A psychedelic yellow with black stripes.
I'm rubbing it, honey;
I'm wetter than rain,
And you're all I've ever wanted . . .
What did you say your name was?
Ray, yeah, that's it.
Now stay with me, baby,
That's right, hon;
Harder, faster, deeper.
Ray groans;
Star yawns.
She's learned she can get away
With a yawn or two if it's perfectly matched
A second after a man moans.
Ray's telling Star what he'd do to her
If she were right there next to him this moment.
He'd do it to her big time.
She's never had it so good, so long.
Star's completed all the toes on her left foot
And gently slides the right one into place.
You're driving me wild with that thing, Star squeals.
I don't know if I can stand it much more.
How do you want to finish?
Ray describes a contortionist's nightmare,
And Star tries to figure out
If the position is humanly possible.
Does Ray have some kind of trouble
With shapes or forms,

Body mechanics or spatial projection?
She reasons that it's his dollar
And the more dollars, the better.
Star peers at the clock on her nightstand,
Then down to her foot—
One toe to go . . .
She likes the new design she's created;
She's not seen it on another foot in town.
Ray's screaming at her now.
Some of his words are unintelligible,
A series of grunts, more or less.
God, I'm exploding,
Star sighs into the receiver,
Capping up the nail polish,
Reaching for the clear coat,
Realizing she's just about out of China Glaze.
Ray's breathing is no longer labored.
Star is not surprised to find
His voice takes on a childish tone;
She pictures him outstretched,
Naked on a bed,
A rattle in one hand,
A sucker in the other.
He thanks her for her time,
And Star tells him to phone again,
Anytime, 24 hours a day.
I'm always here.
I can't remember when I had it so good,
She purrs to Ray,
And then there is nothing
But blank space,
Dead air, silent time
Squeezing through empty wires.

THEY SHOT WOOK KIM

One

Two

Three

Four

Five

Six

Seven

Eight

For thirty dollars,
His only crime
Working at the Texaco down the boulevard,
A long, long way
From Korean fields he fled,
But not far enough, it seems:
Since man is always
At the mercy of other men,
Sentenced by the absence of laughter and love,
All the race has to give.

Yet he could laugh
When something struck him,
Strange American customs
Brought it on.
He often laughed at himself,

Wondering how and why
He'd ended up here.
Complex cultures thrown into chaos,
He'd mutter, shaking his head.

Concerning love,
There was family back home
He was determined to send for;
He owed them everything,
And a brother, here in town,
But the *special love* he deserved
Had not found him.
Perhaps, she's just around the corner, he joked.
A matter of time.

Neither laughter, nor love,
Hung in the air
Over that petroleum morgue that night.
Only a strong wretched odor—
Powder burns and blood,
Vomit and urine.

They

Shot

Wook Kim

PASSOVER (5749)

On Fairfax, near Farmer's Market,
I'm told I should marry.
To grow old is no bargain
They mutter in their long black coats
And nod beneath their yarmulkes,
Noticing how my hair thins;
This is a sure sign of worry.
A wife will calm my nerves.
A full head of hair will be mine
One year to the day
I stand under the chupah.
The holiday just tomorrow:
What am I doing with my life?
How can I pray alone on the Sabbath?
From whom shall I receive nachas?
If not now—when?
They offer to make inquiries for me.

Late evening,
I lie alone,
Searching the darkened universe
For tiny Stars of David
Glittering in the sky.
I dream of endless Seder Plates,
Stacks of Haggadahs surround me,
I cannot reach the charoseth,
The cup I've filled for Elijah
Empties before my eyes,
The Four Questions become Five,
And I behold the Ten Plagues

Spread upon the unleavened bread at my side.
I scream loud enough
To disturb a Pharaoh's nap.

I wake the next day rested
And recite the morning sh'ma.
Dressed in a cobalt suit
I walk to synagogue,
Tallith and phylacteries clutched in hand.
Today's prayer is one of redemption;
God knows my affliction.
Reciting Kaddish,
I ask to be led
Out of bondage from Egypt
Into the land of Israel.

YOU CANNOT KILL ME

We dead don't appreciate sapphire threats—
A knife at the throat,
The twist of a neck,
A blow on the back of the head.

We departed won't listen in our tombs—
A howl from the devil,
The song of a saint,
A curse to snuff out the soul.

We deceased won't walk this wicked earth—
A watch on the wrist,
The scar from a cyst,
A heart in the palm of your fist.

IN AWE OF ELMS

In awe of elms I wait,
A grove away from goodness,
Concealed amidst the lemons and plums,
Awakened by sleep.
This work of mine does not
Disturb the harvest home,
The turning of apples to cider,
A timeless drink.
Beneath the elms I yearn to walk
When first I step upon the soil
And curse the fruit the serpent bore.
Yes, in row after row
These round elms grow,
Spawning skyward over
Green earth gone to seed.
Ah, but all this chatter
Stirs the pot, nothing more.
Content, I count the crop within the crates
Sent forth to cure such addled mates:
Here, Eve washes her sinful stain,
And Adam slinks away in shame.
Gardens bloom among us still,
Mythic wires crossed at birth.
In awe of elms I wait.

ITINERANT HEART

It's not like anyone told you.
It's nowhere you've ever been.
This separation,
This alien station,
A galaxy adrift.
You wish it were merely
Nebulae in the night,
Some iridescent shadow play
Called to another dawn,
But the scent of prey
Never trails far from the lair—
Celestial soil on the soles of your shoes.

Itinerant heart,
Ripe for requiem.
Sail between stars
Locked in consternation,
Astray in endless constellations
Always a planet away,
Searching for some small space
To curl up and sleep
In eternity's embrace.

Still, sirens sound in your world,
Steering you with cutted sight,
The abandoned horizon,
A speck in the universe—
Pilotless craft.
And nothing will bring her back . . .
    Not a photograph,
      Not a prayer,
        Not a promise,
          Not a poem.

A GOOD DAY TO DIE

Sunswept afternoon,
Holy mountains glowing
Orange and blue:
Mother earth,
Father sky,
Eagle's distant call,
Buffalo rumble by . . .
What a good day to die.

Wakan Tanka,
Sacred mystery of the universe,
I give you what I am,
All you have taught me—
The tricks, the trails, the truth.
Drink the river of my heart.
Color this moon,
Stars and sun
With my red soul.

Slowly, your four winds
Enter this empty shell.
Brother turtle,
Carry my dream on your back;
The journey ahead,
Far we have to go.
Seeker of visions
I have always been,
Dancing spirit I remain . . .
Today is a good day to die.

—for Tahca Ushte-Lame Deer

Bart Edelman

SOLITARY APPLE

Resting here, as the sun rose,
Silence crept between us
(Nothing else could fit).
Only the sound of your breathing
Made this house my home.
Suddenly, you awoke with a start,
Knowing I was watching,
Your eyes opened to mine
(Innocent desire before the dance).
You took hold of my hand,
As if there were no other place for us,
But this one bed,
This one room,
This one moment.

It must have been then,
After I'd cradled your head
In the valley of my hands,
Your sighs within me,
I first heard the words,
The precious one syllable notes:
A solitary apple
Dropped ever softly
From your orchard.
I should have picked up
The ripe fruit which fell,
But paralysis set in,
And then another reality . . .
Perhaps, I heard nothing,

Simply my own voice—
One tin can and a string.

Later, you were out the door,
Promises to keep you away,
And the earlier words,
Unspoken or spoken,
Were shuttered, never uttered.
If lost somewhere,
Let it be;
It must find a home.
But should you be passing by
(To bring the morning paper
Or borrow a cup of milk),
And I've done something kind,
A short note would do—
Just place it on the kitchen table
In the basket,
Among the grapes and pears.

THE POETRY OF HATE

Late last night,
One too many Marlboros
And two few shots of Ouzo,
I surrendered myself
To the poetry of hate;
No longer pedaling the soft sob,
The noble cry for the poor
And wailing of the stillborn.
The rhythm of misery my muse,
Syllables in strife,
Across each metric mile I trudged,
Pen coiled, paper ready.

Through hell and back again,
The web I'd spun
Caught them nicely—
From roofs they fell,
Plummeting through clouds of ash,
Ancient pulmonary dust.

As dawn lifted her black veil,
My ledger revealed pages
Forged from silk and iron.
Down tenement steps,
Padlocked belly of the beast,
I lay in the refuge of the mute and deaf:
A silent universe,
Words spoken only by the dead.
When sleep seized me,
I went willingly—
Without a prayer,
Without a name.

JUST THIS

Clear lake,
Azure sky;
This is all there is today.
And wisdom,
Of course—
Suffering's patron saint.
Her shock of flaxen hair
Spills out upon a dressing table,
Steady before the ivory comb;
100 circular strokes,
Morning and evening,
Century by century—
Pure gold spun to silk.
Here is a promise worth keeping,
A reason for rolling the rock,
A one-way ticket fare,
Exile from the Algerian night.
Just this . . .
Nothing more.

Bart Edelman

AT FORTY

At forty I awake:
A fool in a cave,
A sage in a trance,
My life neither backward nor forward,
Pedaling turn after turn,
Mile by mile,
Not uphill or downhill.
In a tiny bare room,
Four windowless walls around me,
Free from weather, nature, people,
I cycle furiously,
Checking my pulse,
Again and again,
Curious habit—
Cautious heart.

At forty I stand,
The misfit in me
Straining for fresh air,
Unsteady on the mark,
(Not part of the clan),
Out of step,
No plans for life's ceremonies:
Vacant altars,
Voiceless choirs,
Hollow vows.
My choices limited—
What can I eat?
How shall I dress?
What should I say?
When will I die?

ASYLUM

I loved you the moment
I saw you standing swollen,
Your round belly
Bearing the seed of another.

I wondered:
Where you lived as a child . . .
How you learned to write your name . . .
Who kissed you first . . .

I never thought
Reason should be
A creature to fear,
Tirelessly travelling
A trail of bedlam,
Asylum to asylum.

But your smile that day,
The way your body swayed,
Made me swim in your ocean,
Crawling from between your legs
When you were ready to unfold me.

Ours is a curious coupling,
Not near or far—
A foot on land,
One foot by sea;
This slow retreat,
Two twigs asleep
In twilight's shadow.

Bart Edelman

One morning,
I will fix you a sandwich,
Iron your favorite dress,
Walk you by the hand to school,
And when they ask me
Who claims you,
We will turn into golden birds
And fly away.

PASSAGES

Dear Bart,

> *I'm sorry*
> *I went to bed sick.*
> *This morning when you called*
> *I was asleep.*
> *Today's Monday,*
> *Gone until 8.*
> *Tomorrow,*
> *Leave at 10:30,*
> *Return at 7.*
> *Wednesday,*
> *Off by 12,*
> *Back home at 9.*
> *In the mornings I write,*
> *You can call.*
> *I need a poem from you*
> *That explains why you*
> *Crossed the Hackensack,*
> *Left New Jersey.*
> *Why leave any life for another?*
> *Why hope movement will shift*
> *Your paradigm of the universe?*

> *The crossing like death*
> *The water dark*
> *You on the other side*
> *Alive, writing*
> *Still wet.*

I need this poem.

> *Love,*
> *Kate*

Dear Kate,

Passages—
Forever shuttle us
Room to room,
Field to field,
River to river.
Voyages create us.
Crossings define us.
Journeys sustain us.
There's an office in my brain,
A library in my heart;
I'm at home in my boots.
Each spring,
Hiking up the trail,
Compass in hand,
Map in pack,
I climb a mountain a day.
Come autumn,
I drift down the Hackensack,
The Ganges, Nile and Vistula.
This is all
There is of my life . . .
I know no other
World for me.
Explanations are like beans,
Better left to Thoreau—
Let him drop them row by row.

When I want something to grow,
I plant my foot upon the earth,
Build a boat to sail,
Draw the wind,
Write a poem.

Love,
Bart

ACKNOWLEDGMENTS

Beatrice and Donald Edelman, who instilled in me a love of literature, reading, and the spoken word.

William Moore, Teaneck High School, my first and only creative writing teacher in the classroom.

Leo Gurko and Frank S. Lambasa, talented professors at Hofstra University, who assured me college teaching was a wonderful way to live a life.

The University of Southern California and the United States Department of Education for awarding me grants to conduct literary research in India, Egypt, and Nigeria.

The LBJ School of Public Affairs at the University of Texas at Austin for awarding me a fellowship to study at Jagiellonian University in Krakow, Poland.

Glendale College for a wonderful teaching career, the opportunity to edit *Eclipse, A Literary Journal,* and the Board of Trustees for granting me a sabbatical to complete work on *The Geographer's Wife*.

David Hakim, at Prometheus Press, who first took me under his wing, urged me to read my work at venues, and published *Crossing the Hackensack*.

Lee Mallory, my first editor and mentor, who diligently taught me the power of compression and how a good poem should sound.

Lightning Publications for having the faith and insight to publish *Under Damaris' Dress*.

Kate Gale and Mark Cull at Red Hen Press for their support, zeal, and direction, while publishing *The Alphabet of Love, The Gentle Man, The Last Mojito,* and *The Geographer's Wife*.

Kevin Rabas, brother and friend, for awakening me out of a deep slumber and encouraging me to take the next literary step forward.

Linzi Garcia and Tracy Million Simmons at Meadowlark Press for their belief and encouragement in my work, these past few years, and their gracious offer to publish *Whistling to Trick the Wind,* as well as *This Body Is Never at Rest: New and Selected Poems 1993 – 2023*.

Susan Cisco, for a lifetime of loyalty, devoting her humor and craft to our collaboration on *Eclipse, A Literary Journal*, as well as providing inspiration and constant support for my poetry.

And Kim, for love and patience far beyond the line of duty . . .

PUBLICATION ACKNOWLEDGMENTS

Many poems in this collection first appeared in the following anthologies, journals, and other publications:

Abandoned Mine Journal: "Fuse."

Arlington Literary Journal: "Consider This" and "This Body Is Never at Rest."

Bryant Literary Review: "Go Gentle into That Good Night."

California Quarterly: "The Song" and "Space."

Chaparral: "The Age of Belief," "All the Pretty Young Girls," "The Dogs of Amadeus," "Little Ghosts," "Maude Tells Claude," "My Song," "The New Train," "Retirement," "Start Here," "When You're Away," and "The Woodpecker."

Chautauqua: "Coastal Lagoon," "Lost at Sea," and "West of the Mississippi."

City Lights Books, in *Another City, Writing from Los Angeles*: "Bed and Brimstone."

Clackamas Literary Review: "Bashevis," "Forgiveness," "In Albany Love," and "Your Father's Ghost."

Coneflower Café: "If Only I Could."

The Dos Passos Review: "Forever Spinning," "Little Daddy's Thanksgiving," and "Poetry Editors."

Etruscan Press, in *September 11, 2001, American Writers Respond*: "Coat of Sorrow."

Exit 13: "Flight 1903."

Flint Hills Literary Review: "The Business of Love," "The Geographer's Wife," "Out of the Country," "Photograph (circa 1960)," "The Potato," "The Rowdy Boys," "So Much Like Marie," and "Voice of America."

Flora Fiction: "Waiting."

The Forum: "Cancer" and "Courtship."

Great River Review: "Enough" and "Mr. Rotundo."

Harcourt Brace, in *Readings for Writers,* Eighth Edition: "English 101."

Havik: "Accident, Illness, Reckoning," "Exit," and "Flat."

Hawaii Pacific Review: "Where Are You, Osbaldo?"

Hobo Camp Review: "Clamor of the Lambs" and "James So Dean."

The Inevitable Press, *Footsteps*: "Black Pearls," "Bones of Silence," "The Book of Life," "The Dancer," "Footsteps," "The Great Dark," "Names," and "White Bird."

Interlitq: "Anyone but Barrymore," "Footnote," "How I Came to You," and "Whistling to Trick the Wind."

Kokanee Review: "Girls Like Linka" and "Raggedy Ann."

Last Leaves: "Patron Saint."

Lowestoff Chronicle: "The Man Without a Name."

The MacGuffin: "Despair."

Main Street Rag, in *Coming Off the Line: The Car in American Culture, An Anthology*: "To Claim the Dead."

The Mochila Review: "The Dead Rise Twice" and "The Dog."

MockingHeart Review: "Erasmus," "Juanita Miranda Montana," "The Last Word," and "The Lobsterman."

New World Writing Quarterly: "Joe Doe," "Resurrection," "Someone Like Godot," "Walter White and the Five Dwarfs," and "What If?"

The Ocotillo Review: "The System."

Orchards Poetry Journal: "Raven."

The Phoenix: "Metropolis of Insomnia."

Poems & Plays: "Colonel Sanders (And the Gospel of Love)," "Frame by Frame," and "I Killed the Poet."

The Providence Journal: "Love Is a Lumberjack with Wings."

The Raven's Perch: "Elements," "In the Life of Earl," and "Reunion."

Revolver Literary Magazine: "The Girl."

San Pedro River Review: "In Heaven."

The Sand Hill Review: "Thin Air."

Shadowplay: "It's a Pig, of Course."

SLAB: "On Finding Someone Who Loved You" and "Pacific Surfliner."

Steam Ticket: "That Was You; Wasn't It?"

Stone Poetry Quarterly: "The Pied Piper."

Stone Table Review: "The Daily News."

Suisun Valley Review: "Equation."

The Summerset Review: "The Wrong Side of Tomorrow."

The Tipton Poetry Journal: "Cat? Bag?" "The Deed," "The Midway," and "Solace."

University of Iowa Press, in *City of the Big Shoulders: An Anthology of Chicago Poetry*: "Hibernation."

University of Iowa Press, in *Red, White, and Blues: Poetic Vistas on the Promise of America*: "Buffalo Dreams."

Wayne Literary Review: "Tunnel of Love."

ABOUT THE AUTHOR

Bart Edelman was born in Paterson, New Jersey, and spent his childhood in Teaneck. He earned both his undergraduate and graduate degrees from Hofstra University. He has taught at Kingsborough Community College of the City University of New York, Santa Monica College, West Los Angeles College, Long Beach City College, UCLA, and Glendale College, where he edited *Eclipse, A Literary Journal*. Most recently, he was appointed to the Affiliate Faculty in the MFA Program at Antioch University, Los Angeles. He was Poet-in-Residence at Monroe College of the State University of New York. His work has been widely anthologized in textbooks published by City Lights Books, Etruscan Press, Fountainhead Press, Harcourt Brace, Longman, McGraw-Hill, Pearson, Prentice Hall, Simon & Schuster, Thomson, the University of Iowa Press, Wadsworth, and others. He has been awarded grants and fellowships from the United States Department of Education, the University of Southern California, and the LBJ School of Public Affairs at the University of Texas at Austin to conduct literary research in India, Egypt, Nigeria, and Poland. In addition, he received National Endowment for the Humanities grants for a series of lectures at public libraries on "The Common Good: Individualism and Commitment in American Life," and "Trails: Toward a New Western History." Collections of his poetry include *Crossing the Hackensack, Under Damaris' Dress, The Alphabet of Love, The Gentle Man, The Last Mojito, The Geographer's Wife*, and *Whistling to Trick the Wind*. He lives in Pasadena, California.

Meadowlark POETRY

Books are a way to explore, connect, and discover. Poetry incites us to observe and think in new ways, bridging our understanding of the world with our artistic need to interact with, shape, and share it with others.

Publishing poetry is our way of saying—

We love these words,
we want to preserve them,
we want to play a role in sharing them
with the world.

Meadowlark Press
— since 2014 —

meadowlarkpoetrypress.com

Follow Meadowlark Press
on Facebook & Instagram

f facebook.com/ReadAMeadowlarkBook

○ @meadowlarkbooks

www.ingramcontent.com/pod-product-compliance
Lightning Source LLC
Chambersburg PA
CBHW021709120626
46545CB00004B/1472